UNDAUNTED QUEST

Book One

The Patience

Michael Timothy Cavanaugh

THE PATIENCE
2017 by Michael Timothy Cavanaugh

All rights reserved. No part of this book may be reproduced without written permission, except for brief quotations in books and critical reviews.

ISBN-10: 1546646663
     13: 978-1546646662

First Edition

Acknowledgements

To my mother, Edythe Louise Kunkle Cavanaugh, my link to twelve generations of Kunkles known by name. I'm proud of my Kunkle heritage and you, Mom. You have been an incredible example of a daughter, sister, mother, and grandmother. You are one of the most truly successful people I know.

To Jack Cavanaugh, a friend of many years and an achieved writer with a teacher's heart. Thank you, Jack, for helping me envision the possibilities.

Also, to my beloved wife, Julie. Your perspectives and insights are treasured. Thank you for the patience and love shown during times when either or both of us doubted this project would ever be finished.

Table of Contents

Author's Note   1

PART I — The Patience

Chapter 1 — *Conflict*   5

Chapter 2 — *To Freedom*   17

Chapter 3 — *The New World*   37

Chapter 4 — *Percy Kunkle*   49

PART II — The Dakotas

Chapter 5 — *Ten Mile Country*   101

Chapter 6 — *Ohio*   109

Chapter 7 — *Belle Plaine*   119

Chapter 8 — *Bachmans*   123

Chapter 9 — *The Homestead*   135

Chapter 10 — *Rinard*   163

Appendix 1 — *Oaklands & Ponsnesses*	183
Appendix 2 — *Byerlys*	193
Appendix 3 — *Lenharts and Harmons*	199
Appendix 4 — *Sons and Daughters of the American Revolution*	201
Appendix 5 — *Wills*	207
Appendix 6 — James Goodwill's *Passenger List*	211
About The Author	215
Endnotes	217

Author's Note

The story of our family is one of converging families from numerous countries driven by religious conflict and undaunted in their quest for a better life for themselves and for their posterity. That quest abandoned kindred familiarity; invited dangers at land and sea; endured war and hardship; in tears buried their old and young; suffered and labored; believed and fought; faced prosperity and poverty; moved, settled, built, endured. Erect as dominos in formation behind us stand hardy stock from various backgrounds, who spoke different languages, were of different personalities, who habited diverse environments and were of varying, Christian faiths. They pushed the next generation forward to a destination seen but through the eyes of God. Each individual of our family is a link in a chain of continuity impacted by those who have preceded them and guided by a powerful, loving God from whom all families derive their name.

Some of us have risen to the heights, others fallen to the depths. In our failures, there is nothing any one of us has done that, but for the grace of God, any one of us could have done. In triumphs, we all share, recognizing no height achieved is made possible apart from those whose shoulders we stand upon. We exist linked in familial community yet individually responsible to God for the life entrusted to us.

Part I of *The Patience* follows the Kunkles of Germany and their related families from Holland, England, Switzerland, Ireland, Scotland, and Norway in their journeys into the New World, many who helped establish the United States of America. *The Dakotas,* Part II, traces the journeys of the Shrivers and related families from their initial settlements in the New World into the adventures of the great American Westward Movement - a movement which began at the Alleghenies and five generations later, with each successive generation of our family moving westward, ended in South Dakota.

It was in the western grasslands of that stark land that the Kunkles and the Shrivers converged into one woman destined for the fertile farmlands of Iowa as told in the story of *The Rock of Molum*.

As our family, many unknown to one another, expanded numerically into the thousands and geographically throughout America and to other parts of the world, the freedom which brought us to America and which we still so desperately cling to today, was tested in the fires of war. *Somewhere in the South Pacific* honors the life and times of one of our own who fell in that great conflagration known as World War II, a war fought against the evil of his day to preserve the freedom of ours.

Strength Instilled is the story of yet another generation of "dominos" pushed from behind by the generation preceding it. *Strength Instilled* captures a way of life now known only in history books.

Two lives from that generation, both raised on Iowa farms, are portrayed in the book, *Weakness Embraced*. Their lives portray the many challenges to faith, hope, and love that face us all in a growingly complex world and our need for a strength beyond ourselves.

The day is drawing near when no force from behind and no momentum forward will link us with the past or with the future. The hour, as quickly as a vapor of breath, the weaver's shuttle, or the life span of a blade of grass before it withers, teaches us to number our days and reminds us we are but dust. The brevity of the moment of welcomed rest, stands in somber contrast to needful and prolonged, thoughtful reflection at the end of life - reflection meant to encourage, sustain, and push forward those who proceed and one day fill the ranks of our family.

Moshe Dayan said it well in his autobiography underscoring that who we are is to a great measure who we were,

> The treads of a half-track rend a slope that has no name and is known to no one: Up comes an arrowhead three thousand years old. Dig again. Into the sunlight emerges a shard from the era of Joshua, the handle of a vessel from which a soldier of Israel once drank. Who was that man? He was myself.

PART I

The Patience

Chapter 1

Conflict

Beginning from Charlemagne's rule (800 A.D.), 61 Emperors of the Holy Roman Empire ruled various European kingdoms at the core, of which, was Germany. By the sixteenth century, under Charles V (the 46th ruler), the Empire began a gradual decline to its ultimate extinction at the hands of Napoleon's armies and the subsequent abdication of Francis II on August 6, 1806, concluding the Holy Roman Empire's 1000-year history.

Charles V was appointed emperor by Pope Leo X, whose extravagances brought the building of Saint Peter's Basilica to an abrupt halt. To make up the deficit in papal funds, Pope Leo X authorized a monk named Tetzel to sell indulgences[1] throughout Europe. Tetzel established a graduated scale of payments based upon social rank and sins committed and issued certificates to hopeful buyers.

A nobleman once asked Tetzel if it were possible to receive a letter of indulgence for a future sin. Tetzel said yes but insisted the payment had to be made at once. The nobleman made the payment, received the letter of indulgence, and the certificate. Sometime later, while Tetzel was traveling, the nobleman attacked Tetzel and gave him a thorough beating with the comment that this was the future sin he had in mind.

A German, Catholic priest by the name of Martin Luther was livid over Tetzel's sales of indulgences, one of Luther's many concerns of the Catholic Church at that time. Driven to spiritually protect the people of his own parish, Luther nailed 95 propositions for Church reform on the Wittenberg church door at noon on October 31, 1517 and in so doing, lit the match for the Great Reformation. Many believe that Luther's one-hour lunch break brought 1,000 years of the Middle Ages, which began at the fall of Rome, to an abrupt end.

Though Luther's intention was to remain within a reformed Catholic Church, he was forced out. German princes followed him and began breaking away from the Roman Catholic Church of Germany. Within two years of Luther's lunchtime protest, Tetzel died a broken man who had fallen into disrepute. While mortally ill and on his deathbed, Luther wrote to comfort him.

By 1520, Luther's writings were being burned by the Catholic Church and in 1521, Luther was brought before the Diet of Worms. 206 people of rank including Charles V, his brother, electors, dukes, archbishops, bishops, abbots, ambassadors, and deputies of free cities were present. Luther's writings were presented in court, and he was told to recant his views. Luther responded, first in Latin and then in German—

> Unless I am convinced by testimonies of the Scriptures or by clear arguments that I am in error – for popes and councils have often erred and contradicted themselves – I cannot withdraw, for I am subject to the Scriptures I have quoted; my conscience is captive to the Word of God. It is unsafe and dangerous to do anything against one's conscience. Here I stand; I cannot do otherwise. So help me God.

Dr. Eck, the moderator of the proceedings, cried above the uproar that the church was a much safer guide to truth than individual conscience. The Emperor rose and left in anger and the next day told his courtiers he could not see how a single monk could be right and the testimony of a thousand years of Christendom be wrong.

Luther was excommunicated after the Diet of Worms and in danger of losing his life, but the German Prince of Saxony, Frederick the Wise, whisked Luther to his Wartburg castle. While Luther resided in the castle under Frederick's protection, he translated the Bible into German and continued his prolific writings. In time, the northern states of Germany were converted to Lutheranism while the southern states remained loyal to the Catholic Church. Many other leaders raised the banner for the Reformation, but it was Luther who best articulated the vision, a vision which ultimately divided the Germany our relatives lived in and would flee from.

As Lutheranism and other religious expressions brought about by the Reformation grew in influence; conflicts, tensions, violence, and extremism grew between them and the Catholic Church. Charles V, the emperor and faithful ally to the Pope[2], had a fanatical zeal to crush the Reformation not only in Germany but throughout his domain and joined with others to target church leaders of the Reformation such as Knox (Scotland), Calvin (French Switzerland), Zwingli (German Switzerland); de Bourbon (Protestants of France or Huguenots); Tyndale (England, executed in 1536), Cranmer (England, executed by Henry VIII in 1556); Groote (Netherlands). These Reformed leaders stood upon the shoulders of pre-Reformers such as Wycliffe (England), Huss (Bohemia or Czech Republic), and Savonarola (Italy).

In 1529, seven years after the Diet of Worms edict to condemn Luther, a second influential church conference, the Diet of Spires, demanded unconditional submission to the papacy. *Sketches from Church History* records the German princes' response,

> The princes were divided; six of them, together with a large number of German cities, declared that in matters concerning the glory of God and the salvation of souls their consciences required them to reverence God above all and that it was not possible for them to yield to the Emperor's demands. Because of this protest they and their followers were called Protestants (page 95).

In 1530, the Augsburg Diet was convened and attended by the Emperor. Before the Augsburg Diet, Luther and his assistant, Melanchthon, drew up a series of articles crystallizing the Protestant beliefs. Luther was still under the ban of the Empire, so Melanchthon represented the Reformed position at the Diet. These articles were called the Augsburg Confession. As a result of this time, the Emperor gave the Protestants until April of 1531 to reconsider their position.

In the meantime, the Protestants formed the League of Schmalkald in order to present a united front to Charles V whose armies were engaged against the Turks and the French. Charles V assisted German Catholics in forming a league of their own. The two German, religious and military leagues, one Catholic and one Lutheran, contended against one another throughout the 1530's yet without war. With Luther's death in 1546 the scales tipped temporarily in favor of the Emperor who had also "eased his schedule" by crushing his French adversaries. Still, he needed Spanish soldiers to enforce his will on the German people and over time, Charles V, weary of war, abdicated.

An uneasy treaty, the Peace of Augsburg, was signed in 1555. It was based upon the idea of *cujus region ejus religio* which means, 'to whom the rule, of him the religion'. In other words, each prince could determine the religion of the people he ruled. If the ruler of a people were Catholic, his people were Catholic; if Protestant, his people were Protestant and, in Germany, Protestant primarily meant Lutheran. And so, through the Peace of Augsburg, Lutheranism was given official recognition in the Holy Roman Empire. The Peace of Augsburg, however, only applied to Lutherans and not to other Reformed ideologies, a fact which 100 years later contributed to the tragic Thirty Years' War (1618-1648).

In response to the Reformation, the Catholic Church convened the Council of Trent at the initiation of Pope Paul III. Cardinals gathered for nearly 20 years (1545-1565) in an attempt to wrestle the moral high ground from the Reformers and to preserve the future of the Catholic Church severely threatened by the Reformation. The Catholic "Counter-Reformation" canonized the Apocryphal books, adding them to the Bible, and reaffirmed their belief that salvation was both by faith and by our good works quoting James 2:17, "Faith without works is dead." This soteriological doctrine contrasted with the Reformed position that salvation was based on faith in Jesus Christ alone apart from works quoting Romans 4:5, "However, to the man who does not work but trusts God to justify the wicked, his faith is credited as righteousness." In other words, to the Protestant, works were a by-product of genuine faith and without "works," or a changed life, there was no evidence a person had genuine faith to begin with. The Reformed view thereby embraced both James 2:17 and Romans 4:5 as perfectly compatible.

The Catholic Counter-Reformation also established the Jesuits as a religious order to aggressively win the world to the Catholic faith. Another outgrowth of the Catholic Counter Reformation was the Inquisition, an approach to identify and try evidence of heresy. The Inquisition's excesses rightly fall at the feet of the Catholic Counter-Reformation rather than at the feet of Christianity per se.

At the beginning of the sixteenth century and prior to the Protestant/Catholic schism, the peasants had a "chicken in every pot." People's optimism in the future led to large families but as the sixteenth century advanced, the German economic conditions became worse. Many peasants witnessed their lands being confiscated by the elite. Homelessness and vagrancy were on the rise. Wages were reduced. Germany was divided and tensions were great between Catholics and Protestants (to whom the Kunkles belonged). Widespread revolts grew as the century progressed. Thousands were slain through religious wars, pestilence, and hunger.

With this history as a backdrop, a man and a woman, unknown to us by name, were moving through life's many challenges toward marriage. As unnamed ancestors before them, this man and woman were born, lived, died, and were buried in the small town of Floersbach, Germany, lying just 40 miles east of Frankfurt, part of the Spessart[3] region of Germany. The man's family name was Kunkle. In 1550, their son, **JOHANNES KUNKLE**, was born. Johannes' wife-to-be, **ANNA ELIZABETH WOLFGANG**, was born ten years later in

1560 during the Council of Trent. Anna lived a mere 35 years, dying in 1595, perhaps in childbirth, for that was the year Johannes and Anna's son was born, **GEORGE KUNKEL**. George's wife, also **ANNA**, was born in 1610. George died at the age of 50 in 1645 having witnessed the foundation Luther laid for the Reformation. As the Kunkles advanced into the seventeenth century, they clung tightly to the only life they had known for generations. They watched many flee Germany for different parts of the world.

As turbulent as the sixteenth century was, the worst was yet to come. A great war in the seventeenth century reduced the total population of the Holy Roman Empire by two-thirds because of war, famine, pestilence, and emigration. Schools and universities were closed, forests replaced fields, 15-20% of the entire German population was killed. Surely many of our own relatives were impacted by this great conflagration.

Germany Showing the State of Hesse

The Thirty Years' War (1618-1648) was a logical outgrowth of the failings of the Peace of Augsburg established in 1555. The Peace of Augsburg declared that the religion of the ruler would be the religion of his subjects. Germany consisted of many small states. Within each state those adhering to the opposite faith of their leader were not given religious freedom. Furthermore, the Peace of Augsburg only applied to Catholics and Lutherans and none of the ever-increasing numbers of German Calvinists and smaller groups of Reformers. Each side had military leagues that had been established and in opposition to one another since the Peace of Augsburg. In Bohemia (Czech Republic) under John Huss's influence (whose statue I've seen in downtown Prague), 90% of the country became Reformed Christians. Ferdinand II was the King of Bohemia and Emperor of Germany and the Holy Roman Empire at that time. As a devout Catholic, he insisted his domains be Catholic according to the Peace of Augsburg agreement and, beginning in Bohemia, persecuted the Christians intensely, a general revolt ensued in which Bohemia renounced their allegiance to him and chose King Frederick in Ferdinand's place. The Battle of White Mountain (near Prague) was fought and won by Ferdinand who then consolidated his control and persecuted the country leaving ¼ of the people alive as slaves – the rest simply disappeared. For all practical purposes, Bohemia didn't exist as a country for another 200 years. Frederick fled to Holland with his wife, Elizabeth, the daughter of King James I of England. The conflict spread to the south and north of Germany. Another decisive battle was fought between the Emperor's forces led by Tilly and the Protestant forces led by the Danish king, Christian IV. The Emperor's forces won.

It appeared the Catholic forces would ultimately gain control until Gustavus Adolphus, the King of Sweden, threw his hat into the ring. Adolphus spoke German, Dutch, French, Italian, and Swedish. He understood Spanish, English, Polish, and Russian with some knowledge of Latin and Greek. In June of 1630 he crossed the Baltic Sea and landed on German soil with 18,000 well-trained soldiers. Tilly opposed him with a greater number of troops and with 30 victories already secured. Germans were hesitant to support Adolphus, especially after Tilly sacked Magdeburg, the one city that

State of Hesse Showing County of Gelnhausen

welcomed Adolphus. 4,000 of 30,000 people were left alive in Magdeburg after the slaughter. Tilly's slaughter of women, children, and men at Magdeburg, however, only served to rouse the passions of the German Protestants against him. From that time on, the Emperor's successes began to decline. Gustavus marched south and met Tilly at the Battle of Breitenfeld. Tilly was wounded and met a crushing defeat with 10,000 of his men taken prisoner. One year later, he challenged Gustavus again and again was defeated. A third battle occurred at Lutzen on November 6, 1632 in which Gustavus was killed, though the battle won. What came to be known as the Thirty Years' War continued for 16 years after Gustavus's death.

In 1648 the Peace of Westphalia was finally signed bringing an end to the Thirty Years' War. This great agreement changed territorial lines, gave Calvinists equal rights with Lutherans and Roman Catholics, and the Emperor abandoned his plan to force Catholicism upon Germany. Protestantism had won the right to exist in Central Europe, but it would be a long time before Germany would recover from its wounds. The Thirty Years' War was over, or put another way, the great European civil war was over but the suffering it caused continued on.

City of Floersbach, County of Gelnhausen, State of Hesse, Germany; Home of the Kunkles

George and Anna's son, **JOHANN (HANS) KUNKEL** was 18-years-old when the civil war ended. He was born in Floersbach in the middle of the Thirty Years' War (1618-1648). His wife's name was **ELISABETH ICKUS**[4]. Six children were born to this union. One of them, **JOHANN SEBASTIAN KUNKLE** was baptized on February 18, 1675 in Floersbach and married **ANNA CATHARINA SAMER** on January 29, 1700. Anna's father was **GEORGE SAMER**. Johann

Sebastian Kunkle died on October 14, 1737.

Johann Sebastian and Anna Samer would have eight children of their own[5]. Johann Sebastian was the last of many generations of Kunkles who were born, lived, and died in Floersbach. His son, **JOHANNES (HANS) KUNKLE,** would be the first Kunkle[6] of our line to immigrate to the New World.

James Kunkle of Denver has made it his life passion to track every Kunkle that left Floersbach. Jim assigned each immigrant and their descendants a book number based on which emigrant from Floersbach they descend from. There were three Kunkle relatives from Floersbach that preceded Johannes to the New World. Johannes, the fourth Kunkle to leave Floersbach, is represented in Jim Kunkle's Book IV of nearly sixty relatives he has traced that left Floersbach. It is through James Kunkle that I have derived most of our Kunkle history. James Kunkle also gave me a copy of Johannes' emigration diary, the subject of the next chapter of this book.

Johannes' lengthy diary of his trip to the New World was a warning to his friends and family in Floersbach not to make the perilous journey to the New World. He believed, after making his journey, it would be better to have stayed in Germany despite the conditions there.

Johannes (Hans) was born in 1709 and married **ANNA MAGDALENA KAISER** (1711) on February 5, 1732 in Floersbach. Anna's father was **MELCHIOR KAISER.** Johannes (Hans) and Anna, like their Kunkle relatives before them, were from Floersbach, but their church family was in the nearby town of Kempfenbrunn where they attended the Evangelical Church still standing today. They lived when Germany was still recovering from the Thirty Years' War.

Hans and Anna planned on setting sail for Lithuania in July of 1747 with their six children[7]. Lithuania may seem like an unlikely destination, but it also had once been part of Germany. Months before their departure, their destination was changed, not an uncommon practice. Instead of Lithuania, they sailed on the *Patience* for the New World, Captain John Brown, master. Their destination was Pennsylvania.

Die evangelische Kirche in Kempfenbrunn. Bild: Kam

The evangelical church the Kunkles attended in Kempfenbrunn

William Penn was born into a wealthy family in England in 1644 but was, as a young university student, expelled from Oxford University for associating with religious "radicals." His father, Admiral Sir William Penn, sent him to Ireland to separate him from this group. In Ireland, however, Penn met and joined the most radical and persecuted of all the Protestant sects, the Quakers. It was this persecution and later imprisonment that drove Penn to seek freedom in the New World for himself and for other oppressed believers, a freedom our ancestors sought as well.

William Penn inherited part of Pennsylvania in 1681 in payment of a debt that King Charles II owed his father. He came to America on the ship *Welcome* in 1682 at the age of thirty-eight and determined to establish his colony as a "holy experiment" – a colony dedicated to religious tolerance. He purchased additional land on the Delaware River from the Delaware Indians. The name "New Wales" was rejected in favor of "Penn's Forest" and since *sylvannia* is a Latin term meaning forest, the name Penn's Sylvannia was chosen and altered to Pennsylvania, a state that would be very influential in many lines of our early family heritage.

Margaret Jasper, William Penn's mother, was from Rotterdam, Netherlands and had many German connections. This relationship may have played a part in why William Penn was promoting Pennsylvania as a haven for the beleaguered German Protestants. William Penn died in England in 1718 but not before creating a destination many Germans sought. Indeed, Pennsylvania flourished as a haven for oppressed religious minorities from Europe. By the mid-1700's, Pennsylvania had become the wealthiest and most populous English colony with many of its citizenry German-Protestant immigrants; many of them our relatives.

Johannes and Anna Kunkle, my 9-great grandparents on my mother's side, made their way to the Maine River and on to the Rhine. They sailed northward to Rotterdam and then to Cowes, England with 122 adult men plus their families, nearly 400 people onboard in all. The *Patience* arrived in Philadelphia on September 16, 1748. Only men and boys over 16-years-of-age signed the passengers' list shown on page 35. Johannes Kunkle wrote one of the most remarkable documents I've ever read, the story of his journey from Germany to the New World and recounted in Chapter 2 of *The Patience*. But it wasn't just his journey, it was also our journey from Germany to the New World.

Chapter 2

To Freedom

Johannes Kunkle's Journal, September 16, 1748

In the month of May, 1748, I departed from Floersbach, Gelnhausen County, my native place in Hessen, Germany, where I sailed the usual way, down the Rhine[8] to Rotterdam in Holland. From Rotterdam, I sailed with a transport of about 400 souls, 122 men and balance of women and children under 16 years-of-age, from other areas of Wurtemberg, Durlach, the Palatine, and Swiss, etc., across the North Sea to Kaupp (Cowes) in Old England and after a sojourn of nine days there, across the great ocean, until I landed in Philadelphia, the capitol of Pennsylvania on September 16, 1748[9]. From Rotterdam, including my sojourn there, I spent seven weeks, caused by the many stoppages down the Rhine and in Holland, whereas this journey could otherwise be made swifter; but from Rotterdam to Philadelphia the voyage lasted 15 weeks.

I have carefully inquired into the conditions of what I describe here, that I have experienced myself and partly heard from trustworthy people who were familiar with the circumstances, the fatalities which I suffered on my journey, and the evil tricks of the Newlanders, which they intended to pay me and my family, as I shall relate hereafter, have awakened the first impulse in me not to keep concealed what I knew of the wretched and grievous condition of those who traveled from Germany to this new land, and the outrageous and merciless proceedings of the Dutch man-dealers and their man-stealing emissaries; I mean the so-called Newlanders, for they steal, as it were, German people under all manner of false pretenses, and deliver them unto the hands of the great Dutch traffickers in human souls. Many Wurtembergers, Durlachers, and Palatines, of whom there are a great number there who repent and regret it while they live that they left their native country, to make this misery and sorrow known in Germany, so that not only the common people, but even princes and lords, might learn how they had fared, to prevent other innocent souls from leaving their fatherland, persuaded by the Newlanders, and from being sold into a like slavery. To the best of my knowledge and ability I hope, therefore, that my beloved countrymen and all Germany will obtain accurate information as to how far it is to Pennsylvania; and how long it takes to get there; what the journey costs; and besides, what hardships and dangers one must pass through; what takes place when the people arrive well or ill in the country; how they are sold and dispersed; and finally, the nature and condition of the whole land.

When all this will have been read, I do not doubt that those who may still desire to go there, will remain in their fatherland and carefully avoid this long and tedious journey and the fatalities connected with it; as such a journey involves with most a loss of their property, liberty, and peace; with not a few even loss of life; and I may well say, of the salvation of their souls.

From Floersbach to Holland and the open sea we count about 200 hours; from there across the sea to Old England as far as Kaupp (Cowes), where the ships generally cast anchor before they start on the great sea-voyage, 150 hours; and from there, till England is entirely lost sight of, above 100 hours; and then across the great ocean, that is from land-to-land, 1200 hours according to the statements of mariners; at length from the first land in Pennsylvania to Philadelphia over 40 hours, which makes together a journey of 1700 hours or 1700 French miles.

This journey lasts from the beginning of May to the middle of September, nearly five months, amid such hardships as no one can describe adequately with their misery.

The cause is because the Rhine boats from Heilbronn to Holland must pass by 36 custom houses, at all of which the ships are examined, which is done when it suits the convenience of the custom house officials. In the meantime, the ships with the people are detained long, so that the passengers must spend much money. The trip down the Rhine River alone lasts therefore four, five, and even six weeks.

When the ships with the people come to Holland, they are detained there likewise five or six weeks, because things are very dear there, the poor people must spend nearly all they have during that time. Not to mention many sad accidents which occur there; having seen with my own eyes how a man, as he was about to board the ship near Rotterdam, lost two children at once by drowning.

Both in Rotterdam and in Amsterdam the people are packed densely, like herrings so to say, in the large sea-vessels. One person received a place of scarcely two feet width and six feet length in the bedstead, while many a ship carries four to six-hundred souls; not to mention the innumerable implements, tools, provisions, water barrels, and other things which likewise occupy much space.

Because of contrary winds, it takes the ships sometimes two, three, and four weeks to make the trip from Rotterdam to Kaupp (Cowes), England. But when the wind is good, they get there in eight days or even sooner. Everything is examined there and the custom duties paid, whence it comes that the ship's ride there is eight, ten to 14 days, and even longer at anchor, till they have taken in their full cargoes. During that time, everyone is compelled to spend his last remaining money and to consume his little stock of provisions which had been reserved for the sea, so that most passengers, finding themselves on the ocean where they would be in greater need of them, must greatly suffer from hunger and want. Many suffer want already on the water between Holland and Old England.

When the ships have for the last time weighed their anchors near the city of Kaupp (Cowes) in Old England, the real misery begins with the long voyage. From there the ships, unless they have good wind, must often sail eight, nine, ten to twelve weeks before they reach Philadelphia, but even with the best wind, the voyage lasts seven weeks.

During the voyage, there is on board these ships terrible misery, stench, fumes, horror, vomiting, many kinds of sea-sickness, fever, dysentery, headache, heat, constipation, boils, scurvy, cancer, mouth-rot and the like, all of which come from old and sharply salted food and meat, also from very bad and foul water, so that many die miserably.

And to this want of provisions, hunger, thirst, frost, heat, dampness, anxiety, want, afflictions, lamentations, together with other trouble, as c. v. the lice abound so frightfully, especially on sick people, that they can be scraped off the body. The misery reaches the climax when a gale rages for two or three nights and days, so that everyone believes that the ship will go to the bottom with all human beings on board. In such a visitation, the people cry and pray most piteously.

When in such a gale the sea rages and surges, so that the waves rise often like high mountains one above the other, and often tumble over the ship, so that one fears to go down with the ship; when the ship is constantly tossed from side to side by the storm and waves, so that no one can either walk or sit or lie and the closely packed people in the berths are thereby tumbled over each other, both the sick and the well. It will be readily understood that many of these people, none of whom had been prepared for such hardships, suffer so terribly, they do not survive them.

I had to pass through a severe illness at sea, and I best know how I felt at the time. These poor people often long for consolation, and I often entertained and comforted them with singing, praying, and exhorting; and whenever it was possible and the winds and waves permitted it, I kept daily prayer meetings with them on deck. Besides, I baptized five children in distress, because we had no ordained minister on board. I also held divine service every Sunday by reading sermons to the people and when the dead were sunk in the water, I commended them and their souls to the mercy of God.

Among the healthy, impatience sometimes grows so great and cruel that one curses the other, or himself and the day of his birth and sometimes come near killing each other. Misery and malice join each other, so that they cheat and rob one another. One always reproaches the other with having persuaded him to undertake the journey. Frequently children cry out against their parents, husbands against their wives, and wives against their husbands, brothers and sisters, friends and acquaintances against each other but most against the soul-traffickers.

Many sigh and cry: "Oh, that I was at home again, even if I had to lie in my pigsty!" Or they say: "O God, if I only had a piece of good bread, or a good fresh drop of water." Many people whimper, sigh, and cry piteously for their homes; most of them get homesick. Many hundreds of people necessarily die and perish in such misery and must be cast into the sea, which drives their relatives, or those who persuaded them to undertake the journey, to such despair that it is almost impossible to pacify and console them in a word. The sighing and crying and lamenting on board the ship continues night and day, to cause the hearts even of the most hardened to bleed when they hear it.

No one can have an idea of the sufferings which women in confinement must bear with their innocent children on board these ships. Few of this class escape with their lives. Many a mother is cast into the water with her child as soon as she is dead. One day, just as we had a heavy gale, a woman in our ship, who was to give birth but could not under the circumstances, was pushed through a porthole in the ship and dropped into the sea, because she was far in the rear of the ship and couldn't be brought forward.

Children from one to seven years rarely survived the voyage; and many a time parents were compelled to see their children miserably suffer and die from hunger, thirst, and sickness and then to see them cast into the water. I witnessed such misery in no less than 32 children in our ship, all of whom were thrown into the sea. The parents grieve even more since their children find no resting place in the earth but are devoured by the monsters of the sea. It is a notable fact that children, who have not had the measles or smallpox, generally get them on board the ship and mostly die of them.

Often a father is separated by death from his wife and children, or mothers from their little children, or even both parents from their children. Sometimes, whole families die in quick succession, so that often many dead persons lie in the berths beside the living ones, especially when contagious diseases have broken out on board the ship. Many other accidents happen on board these ships, especially by falling, whereby people are often made cripples and can never be set right again. Some have also fallen into the ocean.

That most of the people get sick is not surprising, because, in addition to all other trials and hardships, warm food is served only three times a week, the rations being very poor and very little. Such meals can hardly be eaten, being so unclean. The water which is served out on the ships is often very black, thick, and full of worms so that one cannot drink it without loathing, even with the greatest thirst. Oh surely, one would often give much money at sea for a piece of good bread, or a drink of good water, not to say a drink of good wine, if it were only to be had. I experienced that sufficiently, I am sorry to say toward the end we were compelled to eat the ship's biscuit which had been spoiled long ago, though in whole biscuits there was scarcely a piece the size of a dollar that had not been full of red worms and spider's nests. Great hunger and thirst forced us to eat and drink everything, but many a one does so at the risk of his life. The sea water cannot be drunk, because it is salty and bitter as gall. If this were not so, such a voyage could be made with less expense and without so many hardships.

At length, when, after a long and tedious voyage, the ships come in sight of land, so that the promontories can be seen, which the people were so eager and anxious to see, all creep from below on deck to see the land from afar, and they weep for joy, and pray and sing, thanking and praising God. The sight of the land makes the people on board the ship, especially the sick and the half dead, alive again, so that their hearts leap within them. They shout and rejoice and are content to bear their misery in patience, in the hope that they may soon reach the land in safety. But alas!

When the ships have landed at Philadelphia after their long voyage, no one is permitted to leave them except those who pay for their passage or can give good security; the others who cannot pay must remain on board the ships till they are purchased and are released from the ships by their purchasers. The sick always fair the worst, for the healthy are naturally preferred and purchased first; and so, the sick and wretched must often remain on board in front of the city for two or three weeks, and frequently die, whereas many a one, if he could pay his debt and were permitted to leave the ship immediately might recover and remain alive.

Before I describe how this traffic in human flesh is conducted, I must mention how much the journey to Philadelphia or Pennsylvania costs. A person over ten years pays for the passage from Rotterdam to Philadelphia ten pounds[10], or 60 florins. Children from five to ten years pay half price, five pounds or 30 florins. All children under five years are free. For these prices, the passengers are conveyed to Philadelphia and provided with food, though very poor, as long as they are at sea. But this is only the sea passage; the other costs on land, from home to Rotterdam, including the passage on the Rhine, are at least 40 florins, no matter how economically one may live. No account is here taken of extraordinary contingencies. I may safely assert that with the greatest economy, many passengers have spent 200 florins from home to Philadelphia.

The sale of human beings in the market on board the ship is carried on thus: every day Englishmen, Dutchmen, and High German people come from the city of Philadelphia and other places, in part from a great distance, say twenty, thirty, or forty hours away and go on board the newly arrived ship that has brought and offers for sale passengers from Europe and select among the healthy persons such as they deem suitable for their business and bargain with them how long they will serve for their passage money, which most of them are still in debt for. When they have come to an agreement, it happens that adult persons bind themselves in writing to serve three, four, five, or six years for the amount due by them, according to their age and strength. But very young people, from ten to 15 years must serve till they are 21-years-old.

Many parents must sell and trade away their children like so many head of cattle; for if their children take the debt upon themselves, the parents can leave the ship free and unrestrained, but as the parents often do not know where and to what people their children are going, it often happens that such parents and children, after leaving the ship, do not see each other again for many years, perhaps no more in all their lives.

When people arrive, who cannot make themselves free, but have children under five years, the parents cannot free themselves by them; for such children must be given to somebody without compensation to be brought up, and they must serve for their bringing up till they are 21-years-old. They cannot, therefore, redeem their parents by taking the debt of the latter upon themselves, but children above ten years can take part of their parents' debt upon themselves.

A woman must stand for her husband if he arrives sick, and in like manner a man for his sick wife, and take the debt upon herself or himself, and thus serve five to six years not alone for his or her own debt but also for that of the sick husband or wife. But if both are sick, such persons are sent from the ship to the hospital, but not until it appears probable that they will find no purchasers. As soon as they are well again they must serve for their passage, or pay if they have means.

It often happens that whole families: husband, wife, and children are separated by being sold to different purchasers, especially when they have not paid any part of their passage money.

When a husband or wife has died at sea, when the ship has made more than half of her trip, the survivor must pay or serve not only for himself or herself but also for the deceased.

When both parents have died over half-way at sea, their children, especially when they are young and have nothing to pawn or to pay, must stand for their own and their parents' passage and serve till they are 21-years-old. When one has served his or her term, he or she is entitled to a new suit of clothes at parting; and if it has been so stipulated, a man gets, in addition, a horse; a woman, perhaps a cow.

When a serf has an opportunity to marry in this country, he or she must pay for each year which he or she would have yet to serve, five to six pounds. But many a one, who has thus purchased and paid for his bride, has subsequently repented his bargain, so that he would gladly have returned his exorbitantly dear ware and lost the money besides.

If someone in this country runs away from his master, who has treated him harshly, he cannot get far. Good provision has been made for such cases, so that a runaway is soon recovered. He who detains or returns a deserter receives a good reward.

If such a runaway has been away from his master one day, he must serve for it as a punishment one week, for a week a month, and for a month half a year. But if the master will not keep the runaway after he has got him back, he may sell him for so many years as he would have to serve him yet.

Work and labor in this new and wild land are very hard and manifold, and many a one who came there in his old age must work very hard to his end for his bread. I will not speak of young people. Work mostly consists in cutting wood, felling oak trees, rooting out, or as they say there, clearing large tracts of forest. Such forests, being cleared, are then laid out for fields and meadows. From the best hewn wood, fences are made around the new fields; for meadows, orchards, and fruit fields are surrounded and fenced in with planks made of thickly split wood, laid one above the other, as in zigzag lines, and within such enclosures, horses, cattle, and sheep are permitted to graze. Europeans who are purchased must always work hard, for new fields are constantly laid out, and so they learn that stumps of oak trees are in America certainly just as hard as in Germany. In this hot land, they fully experience in their own persons what God has imposed on man for his sin and disobedience; for in Genesis we read the words: "In the sweat of thy brow shalt thou eat bread." Who therefore wishes to earn his bread in a Christian and honest way and cannot earn it in his fatherland otherwise than by the work of his hands, let him do so in his own country, and not in America; for he will not fare better in America. However hard he may be compelled to work in his fatherland, he will surely find it as hard, if not harder, in the new country. Besides, there is not only a long and arduous journey lasting nearly half a year, during which he must suffer, more than with the hardest work; he has also spent about 200 florins which no one will refund to him. If he has so much money, it will slip out of his hands. If he has it not, he must work his debt off as a slave and poor serf. Therefore, let everyone stay in his own country and support himself and his family honestly. Besides, I say that those who suffer themselves to be persuaded and enticed away by the man thieves are very foolish if they believe that roasted pigeons will fly into their mouths in America or Pennsylvania without their working for them.

How miserably and wretchedly so many thousand German families have fared: 1) since they lost all their cash in consequence of the long and tedious journey; 2) because many of them died miserably and were thrown into the water; 3) because of their great poverty, most of these families after reaching the land are separated from each other and sold far away from each other, the young and the old. And the saddest of all this is that parents must generally give away their minor children without receiving a compensation for them; in as much as such children never see or meet their fathers, mothers, brothers, or sisters again, and as many of them are not raised in any Christian faith by the people to whom they are given. For there are many doctrines of faith and sects in Pennsylvania which cannot all be enumerated, because many a one will not confess to what faith he belongs.

Besides, there are many hundreds of adult persons who have not been and do not even wish to be baptized. There are many who think nothing of the sacraments and the Holy Bible, or even of God and His word. Many do not even believe that there is a true God and devil, a heaven and a hell, salvation and damnation, a resurrection of the dead, a judgment and an eternal life. They believe that all one can see is natural. For in Pennsylvania, everyone may not only believe what he will, but he may even say it freely and openly.

Consequently, when young persons, not yet grounded in religion, come to serve for many years with such free-thinkers and infidels and are not sent to any church or school by such people, especially when they live far from any school or church, it happens that such innocent souls come to no true divine recognition and grow up like heathens and Indians.

A voyage is sometimes dangerous to people who bring money or goods away with them from home, because much is spoiled at sea by entering sea water; sometimes, they are even robbed on board the ship by dishonest people, so that formerly opulent persons find themselves in a most deplorable condition.

It avails myself of this opportunity to relate a few remarkable and most disastrous cases of shipwrecks. In the year 1754, on Saint James Day, a ship with some 360 souls on board, mostly Wurtembergers, Durlachers, and Palatines was hurled by a gale in the night upon a rock between Holland and Old England. It received three shocks, each accompanied by a tremendous crash, and finally, it split lengthwise asunder at the bottom, so that the water entered, which rose so fast that the ship began to sink early in the morning. At the last, when the people endeavored to save themselves, 63 persons sprang into a boat. But as this boat was too overburdened and another person reached it by swimming, holding persistently on to it, it was not possible to drive him away till they chopped his hands off. Another person, to save himself, jumped on a barrel which had fallen out of the large ship but which immediately capsized and sank with him. But the passengers in the large ship held on partly to the rigging, partly to the masts; many of them stood deeply in the water; beat their hands together above their heads and raised an indescribably piteous cry. As the boat steered away, its occupants saw the large ship with 30-50 souls still on board, sink to the bottom before their eyes. But the merciful God sent those who had saved themselves in the boat, an English ship that had been sailing near and which took the poor shipwrecks on board and brought them back to the land. This great disaster would never have been known in Germany if the ship had gone down during the night with all its human freight on board.

The following fatal voyage, where all the passengers were Germans, has probably not become known in Germany at all. In the year 1752, a ship arrived at Philadelphia which was fully six months at sea from Holland to Philadelphia. This ship had weathered many storms throughout the winter and could not reach the land; finally, another ship came to the assistance of the half-wrecked and starved vessel. Of about 340 souls this ship brought 21 persons to

Philadelphia, who stated that they had not only spent fully six months at sea and had been driven by the storm to the coast of Ireland, but that most of the passengers had died by starvation, that they had lost theirs masts and sails, captain and mates, and that the rest would never have reached the land if God had not sent another ship to their aid which brought them to the land.

There is another case of a lost ship that has probably never been made known in Germany. That ship sailed a few years ago, with almost exclusively German passengers from Holland to Philadelphia, but nothing was ever heard of it except that a notice was afterward sent from Holland to the merchants of Philadelphia. Such cases of entirely lost and shipwrecked vessels are not reported to Germany for fear that it might deter the people from emigrating and induce them to stay at home.

I cannot possibly pass over in silence what was reported to me by a reliable person in Pennsylvania, in a package of letters which left Philadelphia December 10, 1754, and came to my hands September 1, 1755. These letters lament the fact that last autumn, A.D. 1754, to the very great burden of the country, more than 22,000 souls (there was a great emigration from Wurtemberg at that time) had arrived in Philadelphia alone, mostly Wurtembergers, Palatines, Durlachers, and Swiss who had been so wretchedly sick and poor that most of these people had been obliged to sell their children because of their great poverty. The country, so the letter stated, had been seriously molested by this great mass of people, especially by the many sick people, many of whom were still daily filling the graves.

From 20 to 24 ships with passengers arrived at Philadelphia alone every autumn, which amounted in four years to more than 25,000 souls, exclusive of those who died at sea or since they left home, and without counting those ships which sailed with their passengers to other English colonies, as New York, Boston, Maryland, Nova Scotia, and Carolina, were very unwelcome, especially in the city of Philadelphia but that so many people immigrated to America, and particularly to Pennsylvania, is due to the deceptions and persuasions practiced by the so-called Newlanders.

These men-thieves inveigle people of every rank and profession, among them many soldiers, scholars, artists, and mechanics. They rob the princes and lords of their subjects and take them to Rotterdam or Amsterdam to be sold there. They receive there from their merchants for every person of ten years and over, three florins or a ducat; whereas the merchants get in Philadelphia, sixty, seventy, or eighty florins for such persons, in proportion as said person has incurred debts during the voyage. When such a Newlander has collected a "transport," and if it does not suit him to accompany them to America, he stays behind, passes the winter in Holland or elsewhere; in the spring, he obtains again money in advance for emigrants from his merchants, goes to Germany again, pretending that he had come from Pennsylvania with the intention of purchasing all sorts of merchandise which he was going to take there.

Frequently these Newlanders say that they had received power-of-attorney from some countrymen or from the authorities of Pennsylvania to obtain legacies or inheritances of these countrymen and that there they would avail themselves of the good and sure opportunity to take their friends, brothers, or sisters, or even their parents with them; and it often happened that such old people followed them, trusting to the persuasion of these Newlanders that they would be better provided for.

Such old people they seek to get away with them to entice other people to follow them. Thus, they have seduced many away who said that if such and such relatives of theirs went to America, they would risk it too. These men-thieves resort to various tricks, never forgetting to display their money before the poor people, but which is nothing else but a bait from Holland and accursed blood-money.

Many people who go to Philadelphia entrust their money, which they have brought with them from home, to these Newlanders. But these thieves often remain in Holland with the money, or sail from there with another ship to another English colony, so that the poor defrauded people, when they reach the country, have no other choice but to serve or to sell their children, if they have any, only to get away from the ship. It is impossible, however, to discuss all these circumstances; besides I am sure that the Newlanders and men thieves, on coming to Germany, never reveal the truth about these wretched voyages full of dangers and hardships.

Frequently many letters are entrusted in Pennsylvania and other English colonies to Newlanders who return to the old country. When they get to Holland, they have these letters opened, or they open them themselves, and if anyone has written the truth, his letter is either rewritten to suit the purpose of these harpies or simply destroyed.

From the city of London to the point where we lost sight of Old England, we count 325 English miles; then, from land to land, that is from the last land in Old England to the first land in Pennsylvania is 3,600 such miles, from there to Philadelphia is 125 miles, which makes together 4,050 English miles, or 1,350 German or rather Swabia hours. Three English miles make a Swabian hour, but 25 such hours make a degree, just as the French land miles.

When the ships come near this land, they sail from the Ocean into the Great River. This is a large bay formed by the Delaware River, or rather; it is the Delaware River itself which is very broad there. On the way to Philadelphia one sees on both sides a large flat land with woods here and there. The passage from the sea and the entrance into the Great River is in a northwesterly direction. At the entrance, the Delaware River separates the two colonies, Pennsylvania and Maryland, from each other, Maryland to the left, Pennsylvania to the right. While on the river, we can see much high mountain land, especially the Blue Mountains and on the left hand the tall and exceedingly beautiful cedar trees. At the entrance from the sea the river is so broad that we can scarcely see the land on either side. It grows gradually narrower, and at Philadelphia the Delaware is about 30 minutes wide. There the river, twice every 24 hours, ebbs and flows from the sea. This city lies, as above stated, 125 English miles or 40 hours' journey from the open sea, higher up in the land ... into which most of the rivers of this colony empty; the other waters flow into the other great main river of Pennsylvania which is called Susquehanna and empties into the Chesapeake Bay. In Philadelphia, we can see the open sea through a field-glass.

As soon as the ships cast their anchors in the port of Philadelphia, all male persons of 15 years and upward are placed the following morning into a boat and led, two-by-two, to the courthouse or town hall of the city. There they must take the oath of allegiance to the Crown of Great Britain.

Court House at Philadelphia, in which Oath of Allegiance was signed
(From Drawing in The Historical Society of Pennsylvania)

I, Johannes Kunkle, do solemnly & sincerely promise & declare that I will be true & faithful to King George the Second & do sincerely & truly Profess, Testify, & Declare that I do from my heart abhor, detest, & renounce as impious & heretical that wicked Doctrine & Position that Princes Excommunicated or deprived by the Pope or any Authority of the See of Rome may be deposed or murdered by their Subjects or any other whatsoever. And I do declare that no Foreign Prince, Person, Prelate, State, or Potentate hath or ought to have any Power, Jurisdiction, Superiority, Preeminence, or Authority - Ecclesiastical or Spiritual - within the Realm of Great Britain or Dominions thereunto belonging.

This being done, they are taken in the same manner back to the ships. Then the traffic in human souls begins, as related above. I only add that in purchasing these people, no one asks for references as to good character or an honorable discharge. If anyone has escaped the gallows and had the rope still dangling around his neck, nothing would be put in his way in Pennsylvania, but if he is again caught in wrongdoing, he is hopelessly lost.

The land of Pennsylvania is a healthy land. It has for the most part good soil, good air and water, many high mountains, and much flat land. It is very rich in wood; where it is not inhabited as pure forest, many small and large waters flow. The land is also very fertile, and all sorts of grain grow well. It is quite populous, too, inhabited far and wide, and several new towns have been founded here and there, as Philadelphia, Germantown, Lancaster, Rittengstaun (Reading), Bethlehem, and New Frankfurt (Frankford). There are also many churches built in the country; but many people must go a journey of 2, 3, 4, 5 to 10 hours to get to church.

When someone has died, especially in the country, where an account of the intervening plantations and forests people live far from one another, the time appointed for the funeral is always indicated only to the four nearest neighbors. Each of these neighbors, in his turn, notifies his own nearest neighbors. In this manner, such an invitation to a funeral is made known more than 50 English miles around in 24 hours. If it possible, one or more persons from each house appear on horseback at the appointed time to attend the funeral. While the people are coming in, good cake cut into pieces is handed around on a large tin platter to those present. Each person receives a goblet of hot West India Rum punch into which lemon, sugar, and juniper berries are put, which gives it a delicious taste. After this, hot and sweetened cider is served. This custom at the funeral assemblies in America, are just the same as that at the wedding gatherings in Europe. When the people have nearly all assembled, and the time for the burial has come, the dead body is carried to the general burial place or where that is too far away, the deceased is buried in his own field. The assembled people ride in silence behind the coffin, and sometimes, one can count from 100 to 500 persons on horseback. The coffins are all made of fine walnut wood and stained brown with a shining varnish. Well-to-do people have four finely wrought brass handles attached to the coffin, by which the latter is held and carried to the grave. If the deceased person was a young man, the body was carried to the grave by four maidens, while that of a deceased maiden is carried by four unmarried men[11].

Thus, now in America, we all give thanks to God from the bottom of our hearts, and I kissed the ground with joy, and took well to heart the 107th Psalm which describes the anguish of the seafarers so faithfully. To the Triune God for this great mercy and preservation to praise and thanksgiving rendered now and evermore.

Johann Kunkle concluded this remarkable journal citing a poignant passage from Scripture found in Psalm 107:23-32, 43:

> Those who go down to the sea in ships who do business on great waters; they have seen the works of the Lord and His wonders in the deep. For He spoke and raised up a stormy wind, which lifted the waves of the sea. They rose to the heavens, they went down to the depths; their soul melted away in their misery. They reeled and staggered like a drunken man and were at their wits' end. Then they cried to the Lord in their trouble, and He brought them out of their distresses. He caused the storm to be still, so that the waves of the sea were hushed. Then they were glad because they were quiet; so, He guided them to their desired haven. Let them give thanks to the Lord for His lovingkindness and for His wonders to the sons of men! Let them extol Him also in the congregation of the people, and praise Him at the seat of the elders... Who is wise? Let him give heed to these things; and consider the lovingkindness of the Lord.

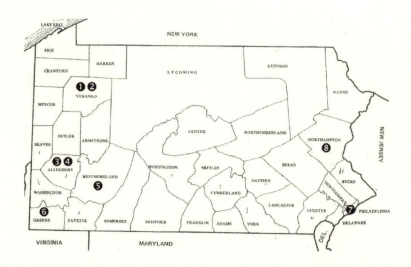

Kunkle family sites in Pennsylvania: ❶ Franklin; ❷ Oil City; ❸ Pittsburgh; ❹ Irwin; ❺ Bushy Run; ❻ Ten-Mile Creek; ❼ Philadelphia; ❽ Kunkletown (named after a distant relative)

Pennsylvania German Pioneers 419

At the Court house at Philadelphia 16
September 1748

Present

Joshua Maddox — ⎱ Esquires
Septimus Robinson ⎰

The Foreigners whose Names are underwritten imported in the Ship Patience John Browne Mas'r from Rotterdam but last from Cowes, did this day take the usual Oaths to the Government

[signatures]

Ship Patience, September 16, 1748,
List 122 C,

Chapter 3

The New World

Having arrived safely, though after a great ordeal, Johannes and Anna Kunkle made their way to Westmoreland County in western Pennsylvania. Their seventh-born child and first of the Kunkles to be born outside of Floersbach was Christina, who was born the year they landed. Anna was at least six months pregnant when they arrived. Christina's brother, **JOHANNES KUNKLE**, settled in Bushy Run, Westmoreland County, where he met another German immigrant and another "Anna," **ANNA MARGARET SCHNEED**. Johannes (Jr.) and Anna married in 1758. Johannes would die on December 22, 1813 in Hempfield Township, Westmoreland County, Pennsylvania but not before he and his wife Anna, witnessed the birth of the United States of America, in fact, contributed to it and bore ten children[12].

JOHANN PETER KUNKLE (PETER), Johannes's and Anna's son born in 1773, died in February of 1830 and married **ANNA ELIZABETH RUCH** around 1795. Elizabeth was born October 30, 1776 and died July 23, 1831. Her parents were **JOHN PETER RUCH** and **MARIA MARGARETHA KOSTER**. Johann and Elizabeth also had ten children.[13]

Johann and Elizabeth's fifth child, **JACOB PETER KUNKLE** was born on January 20, 1803 and married **SARAH BYERLEY LENHART** on February 24, 1833. The Lenharts came from Holland and settled in the Bushy Run area of Pennsylvania, but as with many of our early ancestors who came to America, the Westward Movement began as soon as they arrived. Jacob Peter moved to western Pennsylvania and built his home in Irwin now on the National

Registry of Historic Homes. The stones used to build the house were called field stones. This historic house is about 2½ miles east of Irwin off Route 30. Jacob and Sarah had eight children[14] and shifted the epicenter of our Kunkle family from Bushy Run, Pennsylvania to Irwin, Pennsylvania. I have a picture of their fourth-born son and his wife, my great-great grandparents, Joseph and Sarah (Stewart) Kunkle (page 42). Jacob Peter died May 23, 1857.

Jacob and Sarah's great-granddaughter, Lillie Kunkle, of Nowlin, South Dakota would return to her father's ancestral home of Irwin, Pennsylvania in 1929. She sent her father, Harry, this letter from 5727 Kenwood Avenue, Chicago, Illinois on June 17, 1929 while at school there and shortly after her visit to Irwin,

Dear Father,

Well I should have written you before but just didn't take time to write ... Aunt Lida surely planned the days full. Everyone wanted me to stay longer. Tuesday evening, we went out to the cemetery and saw Grandpa and Grandma's graves (Joseph and Hannah Kunkle), your cousin Frank's, and several others. On the way in, we stopped to see Aunt Pearl and Uncle Harry. We had a nice visit. Their little Betty is quite a girl and resembles Edna so much. We also called on John Ridinger and got some books which dealt with my paper. Also, met Mr. Keister there. They wanted to be remembered to you. That evening also we met a daughter of J. B. Blyholder. Her mother was Katherine Painter, Aunt Lida said.

On Wednesday, we went out to the old home in the afternoon - Hoot (Edythe Cavanaugh remembers hearing of Hoot) and his wife, Phoebe, invited us for supper. She seems like a nice woman and things were clean. I am still puzzled as to why she ever married Hoot. Uncle Taylor is farming some of the land out there and so goes to the country about every evening. He gets back from work each day at 4:30. They eat about then so he can put in a couple hours of work on his crop each day. Paul goes with him and is quite a boy. He is a typical Kunkle in appearance. Sarah is a large girl too and a nice girl - I enjoyed her a lot. On our way, out to the old home, we met Billy Wilson at the Stone House (the one on the National Registry of Historic Homes). He asked about you and sends his regards. He took us into the house over the spring and said we were drinking the spring water the Kunkles for generations back had drank.

On Wednesday evening, we visited with Will Wilson, son of Ephraim Wilson, and he asked about you. Then we went on over to the Bolemans. I had a very nice visit with them. Mr. was so eager to hear about you. He hasn't been able to work since a year ago, January. It is heart trouble. One of their daughters teaches in a technical high school there and the other gave up teaching, took a business course and is a bookkeeper. Mrs. Boleman was very friendly too. I did enjoy my visit with them so much. Of course, I called on Edna and all of Aunt Lida's family. Her mother and father wanted to be remembered to you. We also called on GRANDMA RIDINGER who is in her eighties.

Early Thursday morning we went to East Liberty and called on Anna Hebrank. Aunt Lida had written her so she was expecting us. Her daughter, Maude Troche, was there. We were there all morning and stayed for lunch. I think your Aunt Anna is wonderful. She did tell me so many things about the Kunkles, etc. We had a very good visit. They all thought it terrible that I was to stay only a few days. Then after lunch we went down to the University of Pitt. But their material was limited, so we went over to the Carnegie Library. It had one room devoted just to the State of Pennsylvania, and I did enjoy browsing around. I should like to have remained there a week. Aunt Lida looked up the Westmoreland County biographies while I took notes on my thesis subject. We stayed there until after four and then went to the city. Aunt Lida shopped a little, then we had dinner and went to the theater. Somehow, I was much more favorably impressed with Chicago than Pittsburgh. Oh, while at the Library, Aunt Lida found the data about Jacob Byerly who was a soldier in the Revolution. With the tree traced back to him, I will have no difficulty in getting into the DAR. I'll let you see this in the fall.

Well, on Friday morning we went to the new Methodist Church. It was the final day for Bible school and Sarah and Paul were both in the program. Afterward, Mr. Keister took us through the church. In the afternoon, we went over to Manor. We took the bus over and the street car back, and I got wonderful views. Aunt Lida pointed out so many places to me, and I met so many people whom I do not recall. We called on the Miller's and had a fine visit. Mr. Miller looks like a typical doctor. They asked about you and Ma, also Jim. They told of their experiences in Dakota in '93. Mrs. told about the horse racing on the fourth of July which you will perhaps recall. We had a good laugh, but Mr. Miller didn't seem to enjoy it so much. Mrs. Miller's health hasn't been so good and she is planning to go west, to California. I also met Mr. Will Carson, the messenger, at the station, who said he knew you.

On Saturday, at 8:13 a.m., I left Irwin for Pittsburgh. Waited for a train there about an hour and then rode the whole day and reached Chicago Saturday night. It is nice to be back with the Millers again. I am sitting on the sleeping porch now. Helen Bliss, one of the Sioux Falls teachers, is rooming with me. Well, it is lunch time. There was a letter awaiting me from George when I arrived. Well I must close. Write. With love, your daughter, "Bob."

P.S. I received the two enclosed letters from Sioux Falls while at Aunt Lida's thanks for forwarding them.

In appreciation to his sister-in-law's hospitality given his daughter, Harry wrote Lida this letter on June 30, 1929,

> Dear Lida[15],
>
> Bob wrote me June 17 and said when I had read her letter I should send it on to George. I thought, however, I had better have one of the stenographers copy it, and I shall send you a copy - Bob is a good girl - a close observer and I am sure you will enjoy the letter and the observations she has made. I knew she would be taken up with Aunt Ann Hebrau who she had never met - Bob is back in Chicago and is absorbed in her studies again. I am especially grateful to you, Lida, for getting her to visit Dr. Miller... and above all to look up the biography of Jacob Byerly who was an uncle of Grandmother Kunkle. I had a few lines from Ruth this week - was up on Lake Andes the first two days of the week trying a law suit involving an automobile collision. I shall be able to get out home over the 4th as I had hoped. Give my regards to all our inquiring friends the Bolkmans and others... Bob speaks from her heart - nothing superficial about her.
>
> With kind regards. I am very ...
>
> Harry Kunkle

Jacob and Sarah's fourth child, **JOSEPH JEREMIAH KUNKLE,** married the Scotch Irish, **HANNAH EMMA STEWART** (called "Katie") whose parents came from Northern Ireland. Hannah's father was **JOSEPH STEWART.** The Stewarts lived in the Oil City or Franklin area of Pennsylvania in Venango County. They operated a boarding house whose guests included John Wilkes Booth, according to family oral traditions. His brother, Johnston Stewart, lived in Irwin and had two sons, John and Robert. Joseph and Hannah had nine children.[16] Hannah was the "Grandmother Kunkle" mentioned in the letter above.

Joseph Kunkle and Hannah Emma Kunkle (nee Stewart) with granddaughter, Sarah (nee Kunkle) Forsmark

Joseph ultimately farmed near Irwin but while in the oil area of north central Pennsylvania, he met Katie while staying at her parent's boarding house. They married and lived about eight miles from Franklin, Pennsylvania, the county seat of Venango County and a little farther than that from Oil City, a bigger and better town according to Harry Kunkle. They came back down the river to Pittsburg when their son, Harry, was just two weeks old.

Sarah Forsmark, his granddaughter, described Joseph as having heavy white hair and being very broad and well read. Their home was said to be rigid and highly disciplined. Joseph played the violin, and they had two pump organs in their Irwin, Pennsylvania living room. Sarah said the family was highly respected. Joseph and Katie visited Harry in South Dakota in 1911.

HARRY KUNKLE was Joseph and Hannah's oldest of nine children and my great grandfather and Mom's grandfather to whom Lillie or "Bob" wrote the above letter. Harry sent the following letter to his cousin Sarah Kunkle Forssmark, on June 9, 1944, three days after the D-Day Invasion:

> Dear Sarah,
>
> Grandmother Kunkle's folks lived at Clinton in Armstrong County. Her mother's name was Esther Lenhart and, strange to say, my father's mother's name before her marriage was Sarah P. Lenhart and quite a while after the marriage of my father and mother they (my father and mother) learned that they were second cousins. Grandmother's father's name

was Joseph Stewart and they came to Pennsylvania from Ireland. He had one brother, Johnston Stewart, who was the father of John and Robert Stewart who lived in our old home town of Irwin, where your mother and father lived and where you were brought up. My father went from Irwin to Oil City or Franklin in Venango County and it was there that my father and mother became acquainted. Freeport is the county seat of Armstrong County and on the Allegheny Valley which runs from Pittsburgh on up along the Allegheny River past Clinton and many other places to Freeport and then up to Oil City. They tell me that when my father and others came down from the oil regions they came on the Allegheny River by steamboat as the Allegheny Valley Railroad had not been built and they also state that I was two weeks old when they came out to the Old Kunkle home south of Irwin. My mother's name was Hannah Emma Stewart. This, Sarah, I think, covers the inquires that you have made, and if there is any further light, I can show by writing, shall be glad to do so. I am sending you a copy of the *Sunday School World* which has a general circulation in every state in the Union and which is published at Philadelphia. In the first part of the *Teacher's Monthly* you will find a poem (*Of Sins Forgiven*) of which I am the author. Kind regards to yourself, your husband, and all inquiring friends.

Very truly yours, Harry Kunkle
(Sarah is the little girl with the Kunkles pictured on page 42.)

We're not sure why Harry left Irwin. One report said he moved to Ohio first, met his first wife, then together they moved to South Dakota. I had heard it was because of an asthma affliction but was corrected by Bill Kunkle (Mom's first cousin and Pearl Harbor military survivor) who reported that his grandfather was a robust man who probably came to South Dakota for work opportunities. Upon arriving in South Dakota in 1888[17], Harry Kunkle studied for and passed the South Dakota bar to practice law, which he did in Centerville and then in Yankton. He referred to himself as half-German and half-Irish.

Another account said Harry met a woman while in Centerville and married. Whether they met in Ohio or South Dakota, she soon died of a prolonged illness at a young age before having children. After his first wife's death, Harry married his wife's nurse, **MARGARET J. OAKLAND**. Margaret was 18 and Harry 25. My grandfather, John Percy Kunkle (Percy), the oldest of Harry and Margaret's children, was born two years later. Their oldest five children were born in Centerville, South Dakota, their youngest two on their homestead in Nowlin,[18] South Dakota.

The poem Harry referred to in the above letter was also published in the *Methodist Journal* in July of 1944. It's a beautiful poem to which I've composed a piano score. It speaks of the redemptive story of Harry Kunkle, a capable man but a man who, according to many, treated his Norwegian wife, Maggie, with disregard. She lived alone on the homestead while he lived, first in Centerville and later in Yankton. Harry had a mistress that he brought with him on business trips to Nowlin.

Harry apparently had a spiritual awakening later in life, as the poem below suggests. He spoke of his home as "native dell and mountain" which refers to the Kunkle family home of Irwin, Pennsylvania. This poem clearly speaks of the spiritual conversion of Harry Kunkle and demonstrates he had a great ability for prose. I saw the same strength in his son, Percy.

I think some had a difficult time forgiving Grandpa Kunkle's indiscretions and lack of involvement in Grandma's life. It seems abundantly clear from this poem, however, he found forgiveness from God through Christ for his sin, albeit later in life.

It was said that Margaret called her husband, "Mr. Kunkle" her entire life. Margaret still had a Norwegian accent, according to Uncle Harry and was much beloved by all of her grandchildren, including Mom. Maggie's parents, **JOHANNES J. OAKLAND** and **MARTHA LARSDAUGHTER PONSNESS**, emigrated from Norway.

Harry and Margaret (nee Oakland) Kunkle

OF SINS FORGIVEN
Luke 15:7

(Being the Testimony of a servant of Christ,
a friend of the Union)

There is a place to me more dear
Than native dale or mountain;
A place for which affection's tear,
Springs grateful from its fountain.

'Tis not where kindred souls abound,
Though that is like to heaven;
But where I first my Savior found,
And had my sins forgiven.

Hard was my toil to reach the shore,
Long tossed on ocean of my doubt;
Above me was the billow's roar,
Beneath, the wave's commotion.

Sinking and fainting as in death,
I knew not help was near me;
I cried, "O, save me, Lord, from death!
Jesus, Savior, hear me!"

Then quick as thought I felt Him mine,
My Savior stood before me;
I saw His brightness round me shine,
And shouted, "Glory! Glory!"

O! Sacred hour, O! Hallowed spot,
Where Love divine first found me;
Wherever falls my distant lot,
My heart shall linger round thee.

And as from earth I rise to soar
Up to my home in heaven;
Down will I cast my eyes once more,
Where I was first forgiven.

Left to Right: Erin Cavanaugh; Tim Cavanaugh; Caitlyn Cavanaugh (holding Fiona Cavanaugh); Sam Butcher; Julie Cavanaugh; Jim Kunkle (my fifth-cousin who contacted me regarding Kunkle, family history); Ryan Cavanaugh; Chris Cavanaugh; Sue Butcher; Will Cavanaugh; Edythe Cavanaugh; Chris Siemann; Vee and Cecil Siemann

Chapter 4

Percy Kunkle

On April 18, 1902, Peter Jacobson and Ellen Ritland married and settled near the Bad River in Nowlin, South Dakota. Jacobsons had two boys, Nowlin and Stanley (named after the two adjoining counties). Mom and I met Stanley at a senior center in Midland. He remembered Mom and our Nowlin families and gave me a photograph of his father's sod home, the first house built in Nowlin.

Many settlers, such as the Jacobsons, flooded into "Nowlins" having responded to railroad advertisements encouraging them to "make claim" on a homestead. The local paper, *The People's Tribune*, published its first paper on May 25, 1906. Later that year, a small store was set up at the residence of F. M. Patterson. The Railroad contracted with Norbeck and Nicholson to drill an artesian well at the train station. They hit hot water at a depth of 1,842 feet and 121 degrees Fahrenheit (Mom remembers it steaming all the time). The depot was built in 1907, the same year Harry and Maggie Kunkle (Percy's parents) purchased their homestead while living in Centerville, South Dakota. They called their homestead the Diamond K Ranch whose brand was depicted as a

Harry and Margaret Kunkle

diamond with a "K" in the middle. I don't believe Grandma Kunkle (nee Shriver) named her homestead which she owned and lived on only one year to "make claim" before she sold it. Her brand, however, was "BS" which stood for "Bachman-Shriver," a source of some jest.

Nowlin celebrated the 4th of July in grand style in 1908, complete with fireworks. In 1909 the town initiated a successful movement to build a bridge across Bad River just north of town. The bridge was built in late summer, probably the first summer Grandma Kunkle and her mother moved to their claim. Harry Kunkle also purchased Lot Six of Block One that year from Peter Jacobson according to Book 33 of Deeds, page 359. Harry used this location as a second law office to his Centerville office.

In 1910 the bank opened its doors, and the Catholic and Methodist churches were in operation. On February 19, 1910, Lillie Kunkle (Percy's sister) paid $25 to John Erickson for Lot Seven, Block Two in Nowlin.

While Maggie moved to Nowlin with the children, Harry operated his law practice in Centerville making periodic visits to Nowlin. Some resented Harry for leaving his "Norwegian" wife in the wilds of western South Dakota while he enjoyed the more comfortable lifestyle practicing law in eastern South Dakota.

Harry Kunkle abandoned his wife for a mistress he sometimes brought back to his Nowlin law office. His grandson, Bill Kunkle (a Pearl Harbor vet), fondly remembered staying with his grandfather in the Portland Hotel in Yankton where Harry eventually moved his law practice. He remembered his grandfather kneeling nightly at his bed and saying his prayers *auf Deutsch*. Bill Kunkle didn't think Harry's kids spoke German but said some spoke a little Norwegian.

Maggie Oakland was Mom's grandmother. Mom remembers her grandmother taking her by the hand and saying she wanted to give Mom a gift. They went upstairs in her farm house to a trunk from which a porcelain, Norwegian spoon holder was drawn. Mom, in turn, gave it to me. I attended Grandma Kunkle's funeral with Mom as an infant.

Mom remembers her Aunt Lillie taking her and her cousin, Ruth

Noble's daughter, Margaret Pigalow, to Rapid City for a trip. Mom and Margaret draped their clothes over the staircase of their Grandmother's farmhouse the night before they left, the only part of the trip Mom remembers.

Ruth Noble (nee Kunkle) and brother, Percy Kunkle

Unlike Percy and his family, Ruth Noble and her family were well-to-do. The Nobles had resources. When they moved from Centerville to Nowlin, Harry Kunkle turned the Diamond K over to Ruth and her husband. The cattle that Grandpa raised were also signed over to the Nobles, a source of some sadness and tension according to Mom.

I think Mom sometimes felt slighted by her more privileged cousin, Margaret. Perhaps Mom's grandmother sensed that when she told Mom (who went by Louise as a little girl), "Why Louise, others may have special gifts but so do you, you have a lake named after you[19]."

In 1929, Lillie wrote a letter to her father using his letterhead embossed with: "16-years-experience in the collection business in South Dakota" suggesting he started his business in 1913.

Harry and Maggie's oldest son, **JOHN PERCY KUNKLE,** whom I proudly claim as my grandfather, was born in Centerville on October

2, 1892 and attended school there until the 11th grade. It wasn't uncommon for kids not to finish high school in those days. In fact, none of my grandparents finished high school and, except for Grandpa Kunkle, none of my grandparents went beyond eighth grade.

Percy Kunkle would have been 12-years-old when his father started his law practice in Centerville and 20-years-of-age when he moved with the family to Nowlin.

Percy managed the Nowlin homestead while a young man and with no agricultural training. A wood-frame, Pennsylvania Dutch style home was built on the Kunkle ranch. Near the main home and on the homestead, was a tar-paper shack referred to as "Percy's Place," where Grandpa Kunkle lived. Grandpa was an achieved violinist and provided the music for church and local parties. He attended the Methodist church and earned a stellar reputation as a good man who, according to a neighbor, was very good to his mother. He was also a talented writer as evidenced through his many letters I've retained. Grandpa also began teaching school in Nowlin.

"Percy's Place" on the Diamond K Ranch in Nowlin, with (left to right): Mrs. Heltzel ("Whitie"), Great-Grandma Shriver (left arm paralyzed by stroke), Mary Kunkle, Edythe Louise (Mom), and Mrs. Staley

MARY SHRIVER BACHMAN purchased the general store in Nowlin after "making claim" or "proving up" which simply means she and her mother lived on their 320 acres (two 160's) one year to qualify for ownership of the land. The land was sold and the store in Nowlin was purchased and later burned down. To make matters worse, the insurance company had gone broke, and Grandma lost her entire homesteading investment.

Grandma and Grandpa were active Methodists and separated in age by ten years. They were married December 29, 1914. Grandpa was 22 and Grandma was 33.

Grandma Kunkle (Margaret Oakland) at the Kunkle, Diamond K Ranch. Lillie's room is the upstairs window. The upstairs "long room" ran the length of the house. The nearby well reduced the distance to carry water.
The car was purchased by an inheritance John Oakland gave Maggie.

Regarding Grandpa and Grandma's marriage, the official paper of Turner County, *The Journal,* Vol. 29, No. 1, reported in an article entitled, "Well Known Young Man Married at Rapid City, December 29, 1914,"

> A couple of weeks ago the editor of *The Journal* received word from Percy Kunkle, a former Centervilleite, now located at Nowlin, S. D., telling us he was soon to be married to the sweetest girl in the

world but cautioned us not to say a word until the event has transpired. The knot is now tied, and we can now state that Percy was married on December 29, 1914 at Rapid City, to Miss Mary S. Bachman of Nowlin. *The Journal* wants to extend its sincere congratulations to the young couple. We have not the acquaintance of the bride, but she must be a prize worth winning or our Percy would not have fallen a victim. To the lucky young lady, we want to say she is indeed most fortunate in the choice of a husband, for no more manly or upright young man ever walked in shoe leather than Percy Kunkle. A Christian young man of high ideals, industrious, and ambitious, he is sure to succeed and make a happy home for the lady of his choice.

The article said that Grandpa and Grandma went to Rapid City on the railroad and were married at the minister's home (Reverend D. E. Matteson). Grandpa was cited as being a school teacher in Nowlin. Grandma was cited for her philanthropic work having helped a young boy receive a needed operation curing his clubbed-foot.

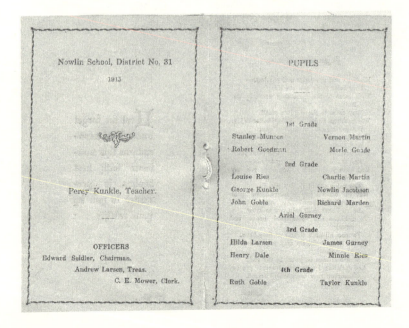

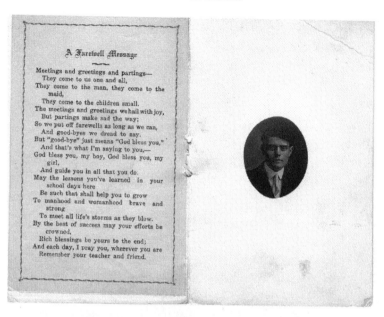

Percy Kunkle's farewell message to his elementary classes. His brothers, George and Taylor, were among his students.

Mom was born December 8, 1915 and Harry five years later, in 1920. Percy and Mary tried to ranch in Nowlin but ultimately moved to Lead to make it financially.

Grandpa moved from their tar-paper shack in 1926 and acquired a job working at the Homestead Gold Mine in Lead. Mom was 10-years-old that summer.

There was a farewell party for the Percy Kunkle family set for Monday, July 19, 1926 at the Community Hall. Ice cream and cake was served. Before they moved to Lead and in anticipation of more income, Grandpa and Grandma purchased a washing machine and a sewing machine. I don't think the income was as forthcoming as they hoped.

Grandma and Grandpa moved to 803 Searle Street in Lead, South Dakota. Stanley Jacobson said they were among many from Nowlin that moved to Oregon, Washington, and California in the late 1920's and 1930's bringing Nowlin's brief period of promising growth to a drastic halt.

Nowlin is a ghost town today. One of the few landmarks left in the community is the 25-acre graveyard outside of town on land donated by Harry Kunkle. Harry Kunkle, his wife, and many of his children are buried there. Within view of the cemetery is the old Noble business, the Squaw Cooler, Harry's oldest daughter, Ruth, and her husband's service station/restaurant.

While in Lead, Mom secured a job cleaning a home next to the school. Grandma purchased a potato chip machine and sold potato chips to help supplement family income. Grandpa disliked descending into the bowels of the earth at the Homestake Gold Mine (nearly 3,000 feet) but persevered for several years with Grandma's efforts at sprucing up his lunches to give him something to look forward to. In time, however, he began to look for different work.

Four years after moving to Lead, Grandpa gave up the mine and a brief stint of selling cosmetics and moved to Yankton, South Dakota to work in collections for his father. Grandma remained in Lead until June of 1930 when she learned of a temporary job opportunity in Rinard, Iowa working as a postmistress. Her brother, Andrew Shriver, worked in Rinard with the railroad and gave her the job tip. Grandma contacted Grandpa and asked what he thought about her moving to Iowa. Grandpa told her that the collection business was not working out, and it would be best if she took the job. Grandpa continued to live in Yankton and worked for his dad while Grandma and the kids moved to Rinard, Iowa.

Meanwhile, Grandpa's brother Taylor moved to eastern South Dakota to earn a living but apparently had difficulty doing so, he returned to Nowlin and in depression shot himself with his brother Montrose's .22 caliber rifle. Bill Kunkle, Montrose's son, told me that when his father learned that his rifle caused his brother's death, he smashed the rifle against a fence post. Taylor shot himself in the forehead at Percy's Place, the home Mom lived in until she moved to Lead at ten years-of-age. Mom felt badly that Great Grandma Kunkle was taken to see Taylor's body. Great Grandma Kunkle was a very tender hearted, loving, and hard working person, according to Mom. Mom loved her grandmother Kunkle very much. Taylor was laid out

Mary (nee Shriver) and Percy Kunkle in front of the Rinard, Iowa post office Grandma managed

in a casket on the south porch of his mother's home at the Diamond K Ranch. People could pass the casket and enter the home's living room from a door off the porch, a feature of Pennsylvania Dutch homes.

Bill Kunkle said his grandmother lived a difficult life and spent much time alone while his grandfather lived in a nice hotel room in Yankton. Grandma Kunkle raised chickens and traded eggs for flour in Philip. Bill remembers her always wanting to fry him eggs and "pannie" cakes.

Eleanor R. Zimmerman, Ruth (Kunkle) Noble's daughter wrote this account of Grandma Kunkle (Oakland) in October 24, 2006. She said that she remembered her grandma sitting at her table with a light from the kerosene lamp reflecting on her face as she read her Norwegian Bible. Eleanor added, "A shine in her eyes, and the look on her face, to me was beauty. It was peace, love, and security to me. Perseverance first and strength kept her continuing as she faced the many hardships of a woman alone, living on the prairie farm of South Dakota." She continued,

> Her skin, wrinkled and dried from sun and wind as she did her many farm chores, was another dimension of her character. Her hair, referred to as a woman's crowning beauty, had never had color added or removed. Every morning, whether it was blazing hot or forty degrees below zero, Grandma went outside to brush her hair 100 strokes, sometimes brushing cornmeal in it to combat the dryness, then it was twisted and pinned in a "knot" on top of her head.
>
> I loved feeling Grandma brush my hair and felt grown-up with a "knot" rather than "pig-tails" (as braids were called). We'd hurry back inside her small kitchen, to warm ourselves by the stove, as she fried "panny cakes" and eggs. After we said the Norwegian table grace, we'd eat together and drink a cup of coffee, which was "strong enough to curl your hair"! Grandma taught me to put the sugar lump under my tongue, then sip the coffee through it, as was her Norwegian custom.
>
> In those days, if a woman was slim, it meant her husband was a poor provider. Grandma wrapped her body with strips of cloth so she would give the appearance of being "well-fed" so as not to disgrace her husband.
>
> Carrying water from the well, pumping water for the animals – all the many farm chores – from feeding and cleaning up after animals to tending a huge garden, gave Grandma plenty of exercise. She didn't need a treadmill or membership in an exercise club! Chasing pigs out of the garden promoted endurance!

Grandma's house always smelled like a bakery as she baked breads, biscuits, and cookies. And when she hugged me, to comfort me, I smelled vanilla, which was her only perfume. In my memory, it was far better than the most expensive ones you can buy today. Her comforting arms holding me, whether I was "homesick" or recovering from a bee sting, left a memory I feel today.

Grandpa didn't own a car, and his visits to Iowa became fewer and fewer. From time to time, he borrowed his brother, Richard or "Birdie's" car to see the family now living in Rinard, Iowa. Mom recalls Grandpa taking her to a fair in Sioux City and riding the roller coaster with him. Sometimes Mom expected him home when he didn't show up.

In Yankton and while working for his dad, Grandpa moved into Judge Boyle's home (a friend of his father) with a brother and several single men. The Depression continued to cripple Grandpa; he was separated from his family; he had limited funds; no car; his father was his boss; he was approaching 40 but with little prospect for success; he lived with single men at his father's friend's home; his younger brother and one-time student, George, attended Vanderbilt then Yale and was an achieved attorney working with his father; Taylor had committed suicide; and Grandpa was struggling to meet financial obligations. The pressure was too great and Grandpa snapped in one unfortunate act of desperation on Saturday, August 26, 1933 in Springfield, South Dakota which tarnished his otherwise stellar reputation.

Sue Butcher relates the story of her return to Nowlin and visiting with a blind neighbor of Grandpa and Grandma's. This blind neighbor recognized Sue as having the same voice as Grandma Kunkle and then proceeded to tell Sue that Grandpa robbed the bank, the first Sue heard of it. She told Sue that when she and her husband heard that Grandpa was in prison for robbing a bank, her husband and a friend drove a horse-drawn wagon from Nowlin all the way to Yankton, which is on the other side of the State. They were so sure he was innocent and planned to return with him. When they arrived and spoke to Grandpa, he simply said, "Go home, I did it."

From the Thursday, August 31, 1933 *Tyndall Tribune* article, "Springfield Bank Robbed; Lone Bandit with Gun Gets $900 in Cash Saturday and Makes Safe Getaway," we read,

> A lone bandit held up the Springfield state bank about 3 o'clock Saturday afternoon and escaped with between $900 and $1,000 in currency unnoticed by the shopping crowd on the street, having two of the bank's officers in the closed-up, unlocked vault.
>
> The bandit was driving a dark blue Model A Ford, the license plates of which were covered with paper. This latter fact, and the appearance of the stranger, had attracted some attention on the streets earlier in the day and even aroused some suspicion.
>
> He was described as about 5' 8" in height, around 35-years-of-age, was wearing dark brown unionalls (coveralls) and a gray hat and wore dark glasses.
>
> Several people reported having seen the man driving around on the streets during the day, and Walter O'Donnell and another man undertook to follow him, their suspicions aroused by the covered license plates. They lost track of him, however, as did others who reported having seen him.
>
> The bandit had apparently driven south toward the new swimming pool and then circled to the west, parking his car on the west side of the bank near the front. Dr. H. A. Fitzgerald (dentist) with offices over the bank saw the car parked there and noticed it was occupied by a strange man apparently reading a paper.
>
> At the time, no customers were in the bank, the man entered, Mrs. Vina Kibble, bookkeeper, was alone at the counter. He flashed a gun and ordered her into the back room, with hands up, where E. B. Dwight, cashier, was working, and Dwight also was forced to hold up his hands.

The bandit then forced them back to the front room and told them to lower their hands, apparently so that the suspicions of any passerby would not be aroused. He scooped up all currency in sight on the counter and rifled the cash drawer. Then he ordered Dwight to open the safe in the vault, but Dwight told him it was locked with a time lock. Sharply he asked Dwight if he was telling the truth, and Dwight assured him he was, and the bandit did not press the matter further.

He hustled Dwight and Mrs. Kibble into the vault and shut the door but did not lock it. In about ten minutes the two had effected their escape but by that time the robber and disappeared with his car. Apparently, he was not noticed by people on the street as he came out of the bank and drove away, even by men sitting in front of the building next door or those across the street.

As soon as the alarm was given, notice was sent out to officers in all towns in this section. It is not believed the man had a confederate. He was alone when seen prior to the robbery by those whose intention had been drawn to him.

No further clues have been uncovered, at this time, as to the identity of the hold-up-man, or as to his whereabouts. He is said to have talked very little in the bank, directing the officers for the most part by motions with his gun.

After the robbery, Grandpa headed north a few miles on Highway 37, then turned east on Highway 52 to Yankton, which was just 30 miles away. In route, he threw his clothing out the window into a ditch. His name was inscribed in his hat, and his initials "P. K." were on his handkerchief. I spoke with a lady from the Springfield historical society in 2012. She well knew the story and said it was one of her relatives that found Grandpa's clothing.

Forty-five days passed before Grandpa was arrested at his

residence in Yankton at the age of 41. He spent 4 days in jail in Tyndall. He pled guilty simply saying, "I held up the bank at Springfield." The Thursday, October 12, 1933 *Tyndall Tribune* reported,

> "Kunkle Given 10 Year Penalty;
> Percy Kunkle of Yankton is Given Maximum
> Sentence
> for Robbery of Springfield Bank"
>
> Percy Kunkle, who was arrested last Monday evening at Yankton in connection with a robbery committed at Springfield, South Dakota, on August 26, and who has since been held in custody at Tyndale, was taken before Judge A. B. Beck at Lake Andes this Thursday morning and found guilty to a charge of grand larceny. This offense under South Dakota law carries a maximum sentence of ten years in the State Penitentiary. He was given the maximum sentence of ten years and will perhaps be taken to Sioux Falls to commence serving this term on Friday of this week. Accompanying Percy Kunkle to Lake Andes was one of his attorneys, George Kunkle, Sheriff John Daub and Deputy State Attorney, Henry Halla, of Tyndall.
>
> Sheriff John Daub, Deputy States Attorney Henry Halla, and Jack Kirwan motored to Yankton Monday evening to bring back Percy Kunkle, of that city, who was arrested there and is being held in the Bon Homme county jail for questioning as a suspect in the robbery of the Springfield State Bank on the afternoon of August 26.
>
> Kunkle, who had been under suspicion for several weeks, was arrested soon after his return to Yankton from an extended trip. He had not been in the city for several weeks and officers had been on the lookout for his return.
>
> He was arrested Monday evening as he was leaving

the home of County Judge Virgil Boyles in north Yankton where he had gone soon after his return to the city. He had intended to take up his residence there, he said. His brother and several other young men have been rooming at the Boyles' home.

Kunkle had been under suspicion for several weeks following the discovery of a hat, a pair of coveralls, a pair of dark glasses and a handkerchief, apparently tossed out of a car by someone in haste, near the Mike O'Donnell farm several miles north of Springfield on the highway.

The coveralls corresponded to the pair the lone bandit was wearing during the robbery. The handkerchief found in a pocket of the coveralls bore the initials "P.K." and the hat had, in addition to the initials, the full name "Percy Kunkle" within the hat band. The car driven by Kunkle also corresponds to the description of the bandit car.

Following his arrest Monday evening, he was searched and a handkerchief, identical to that found in the coveralls, was in his pocket. The local officers said Kunkle and only about $2.50 on his person when arrested.

No definite time has been set for the hearing, at this time, but it is expected that it may be held sometime this Thursday. Witnesses from Springfield will be called at the time of the hearing in an attempt to identify him.

The *Yankton Press & Dakotan* of Wednesday evening reported:

Kunkle had no knowledge of the finding of a hat with his name in it or of the finding of a handkerchief with his initials in the coveralls or of the other details which built up a chain of circumstantial evidence that led to his arrest, his brother, George Kunkle, said today. The latter, an attorney, talked with his brother at Tyndall Tuesday. George also said this morning that Percy told him he had been collecting for his father, an attorney and collector here, the afternoon that the bank was robbed and that he had not been in the vicinity of Springfield. He gave George the names of several persons with whom he had talked and the latter said today that he intended to get in touch with them to check the story.

He also said that his father's diary showed that Percy was in Yankton at 4 o'clock Saturday afternoon, August 26. The bank was robbed about 3 o'clock.

Harry Kunkle, Yankton attorney, and father of the suspect states that Percy has a wife and two children at Rinard, Iowa. Mr. Kunkle said that he did not know of the movements of his son during the period in question and had seen or heard nothing to indicate any connection with the Springfield robbery. Mr. Kunkle has for many years operated a collection agency in Yankton and Percy has, during the past several years, assisted his father in the work.

The bank at Springfield was robbed on Saturday afternoon, August 26, by a lone bandit who wore a new pair of striped coveralls and a pair of dark glasses. He was described as being of medium height, light build, and about 35-years-of-age. He was driving a model "A" Ford sedan, dark blue or black in color. His license plates it was said by several had been covered with paper.

The bandit entered the bank shortly before closing time, scooping up between $900 and $1,000 in cash, shut E. B. Dwight, cashier, and Mrs. Vinta Kibble, bookkeeper in the vault and left without being observed by persons on the street.

He had been seen about the town during the day by several persons. The suspicions of some of the observers had been aroused and he had been followed about the city but apparently had disappeared just before the robbery.

An official statement said that he took $1,078, entered a plea of guilty and was sentenced to a term of ten years in the State penitentiary. The official statement further stated,

> The defendant was never in any trouble before and has always borne a good reputation. He comes from a good family and is not regarded as a real criminal. We are satisfied that this is the defendant's first job and that he is not the type of man that will develop into a professional gun man or robber ... signed by Judge Beck, the clerk of court, and Henry Halla, state attorney. It said that his associates were "very good"; his habits, "very good"; his reputation, "very good" and that he had never been in prison before. He was arraigned in the First Judicial County of Bon Homme County.

On October 12, 1933, Grandpa was sentenced for his crime. L. A. Stekly and A. B. Beck also signed the statement of the Court,

> The plea was received by the Judge and the defendant found guilty as charged. The defendant was then informed of the nature of the information, his plea of guilty, the finding of the Judge, and was asked if he had any legal cause to show why judgment should not be pronounced against him, and no sufficient cause being alleged or shown, the Court thereupon pronounced the following Judgment and Sentence: And now upon this 12th day of October, 1933, it is by the Court considered, ORDERED AND ADJUDGED that the defendant, Percy Kunkle, be imprisoned in the State Penitentiary of the State of South Dakota at Sioux Falls, in Minnehaha County, in said State, at hard labor for the full term and period of ten (10) years, there to be kept, fed, and clothed according to the rules and

discipline governing the said penitentiary. The said defendant stands committed to the custody of the Sheriff of said county pending the execution of this sentence and judgment. Dated this 12th day of October, 1933.

I, L. A. Stekly, Clerk of Circuit Court in and for said County and State, do hereby certify that the annexed and foregoing paper is a full, true, correct, and complete copy of the original "Sentence of the Court." In witness, whereof, I have hereunto set my hand and affixed the official seal of said Court at Tyndall, South Dakota, this 12th day October, 1933.

Grandpa's prolonged depression (perhaps like Taylor's) culminated on that fateful day of August 26, 1933 in an unfortunate, uncharacteristic act that would hang over his life for many years to come. It's true of us. One wrong choice can potentially have long reaching and unfair consequences.

When entering prison, Grandpa turned in one watch (Ingrahm) and $2.47. All his clothes were destroyed. Grandpa weighed 158 pounds and signed a note authorizing the warden or his authorized representatives to open and examine all correspondence in or out of the prison while incarcerated at the South Dakota State Penitentiary in Sioux Falls. He was admitted on October 13, 1933 as prisoner #7222.

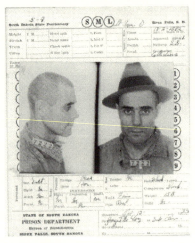

We learn from Grandpa's admittance record that he drank and smoked but did not chew. He was cited as living in Rinard since June of 1930 but grew up in South Dakota all his life. His father, Harry, was identified as German/Irish and his mother Maggie as Norwegian. His prison record further states he had gone through 11th grade, was 20 when he left Centerville and that he was a Methodist. Grandpa met Mildred Santee of South Sioux City, Iowa nine months prior to the robbery. Upon his admittance into the prison, she was listed as his "sweetheart."

One man later wrote of Grandpa's mental condition at this time:

October 26, 1933

> In a talk with Harry Kunkle, and from a naturally sympathetic feeling which any lawyer should have for another, I discussed with him, on my own motion, the procedure which was followed in the transfer of H. D. McCain from the penitentiary to the Insane Hospital here at Yankton, shortly after McCain was committed as a defaulting County Official of this County. By the action of the Board of Charities and Corrections after the matter had been called to their attention, McCain was sent to the insane asylum for examination and observation, and he is there yet, notwithstanding the fact that he was fully pardoned a long time ago.
>
> There has been a feeling among those with whom he had contact, and particularly Yankton lawyers, that for a long time, there was something of a nervous or mental ailment afflicting Percy Kunkle, recently committed to your institution from Bon Homme County.
>
> On a trip to Sioux Falls, it had been my purpose to call on you and discuss this situation, but we had two break downs and did not reach Sioux Falls, and the matter which was taking me there, was otherwise handled.
>
> In the McCain case, we ran into quite a lot of opposition from the then warden, but the board, and the specialists, who included Dr. Adams, and Dr. Wellsite, together with a specialist from Sioux Falls, advised the transfer.

> I am not anticipating that you would oppose such a transfer, if the mental condition of the inmate justified the same, and I am wondering if you would let me have your reaction to this suggestion.
>
> Very truly yours, James Meighen, Attorney at Law, 203½ West 3rd Street; Yankton, South Dakota.

This response was sent to Meighen two days later, on October 28, 1933,

> My dear Sir:
>
> Replying to your letter of October 26 relative to Percy Kunkle, I can only say this, Mr. Meighen, that Mr. Kunkle has not been in this institution a sufficient period of time for me to have come in direct contact with him and from the subject such as your letter suggests, don't feel that I would be competent to judge. However, let me say this to you that if Mr. Kunkle is in the condition of mind that your letter indicates might be the case, you can rest assured that there would be no opposition by me to his being placed where he might receive proper treatment for such a condition.
>
> Yours very truly,
> Eugene Reiley, Warden

Apparently, any possible incrimination against Grandpa's mental health was quickly dropped (though he clearly was under extreme duress during those days) and not brought up by any other source that I am aware of. People saw Grandpa for the man they knew him to be, a good and decent man who had a lapse of judgment under extreme duress for a long period of time.

Having lived in Yankton for nearly three years while working for his dad, Grandpa must have gotten to know many of his father's legal friends. Sheriff Daub was a friend from Tyndall, South Dakota. Grandpa's siblings at the time included Montrose (Box Elder), George

(Yankton), Richard (Nowlin); Ruth (Nowlin); and Lillie (Sioux Falls).

Grandpa entered prison on October 13, 1933 and the first letter he wrote was to Mildred Santee of South Sioux City, Iowa on October 15. She lived at 327 East 11th Street, South Sioux City, Iowa. He would write Mildred ten more letters from October 15 through December 31, 1933. During that same time, he wrote eight letters to: Uncle Harry (10/22); brother George (10/22, 29); his father (10/22); Montrose or "Ole" (10/22); and Mom (11/5, 11/19, 12/3). Mom wrote four letters to Grandpa during that time.

Grandpa received two letters from Grandma Mary Kunkle, one on October 20 and one on December 25, 1933. He received a letter from Mildred on October 21 and 11 more by December 28, 1933.

Grandpa wrote Mildred 50 letters in 1934, and she wrote Grandpa 43 letters. Mom wrote Grandpa 26 letters from Rinard and four from Morningside College in the fall of 1934. The prison didn't keep the letters, they only accounted for which ones Grandpa received and sent. Grandpa wrote Uncle Harry one letter on December 24. Judge Beck wrote Grandpa a letter on December 24.

In 1935, Mildred wrote 33 letters to Grandpa, and he wrote her 46 letters. Mom was attending Morningside College and living at 1201 South Glass Avenue in Sioux City where she received 28 letters from Grandpa that year and wrote Grandpa 46 letters. Uncle Harry received 19 and sent ten. Notably, Grandpa never wrote Grandma a letter while in prison, though she wrote him three letters in the initial months of his incarceration.

Grandpa wrote Mildred 19 letters spread out over 1936. His last letter to her was December 28, 1936, over six months since she last wrote him (June 13, 1936). Mom received 31 letters from Grandpa in 1936 and 45 in 1937. Uncle Harry received two letters in 1936 but nearly 24 in 1937. Grandma wrote another letter to Grandpa on May 9, 1936. Oddly enough, when he wrote to his father, whether Harry was in Phillip, Yankton, or Nowlin, Grandpa identified him, in the prison record as his brother.

Grandpa wrote Mom 50 letters in 1938 while Mom lived in Lohrville. Dad probably sorted those letters into Mom's mail box since he was working at the post office then. Uncle Harry received 17 letters. Grandpa usually wrote both Mom and Uncle Harry on the same day.

Mom wrote Grandpa 39 letters in 1937, far more than anyone. His father sent Grandpa nearly a letter a month, 11 total. Perhaps Grandpa's incarceration played into his father's redemptive story captured in Harry Kunkle's poem published in 1944, *Of Sins Forgiven.*

Grandpa's last letter was written to the attorney in Sisseton, South Dakota on April 31. He received two letters on April 10, one from Mom and the other from Montrose.

From October of 1933 until April of 1939, Grandpa wrote Mom 200 letters, and she wrote him 215 letters. Grandpa wrote Blondie 115 and received 107 letters from her. Apart from Mom and Blondie, Grandpa wrote to all others a total of 164 letters and received 263. In total, Grandpa wrote 479 letters and received 605 letters in the 67 months he was in prison.

As Grandpa's fifth-year anniversary drew closer, on June 19, 1938, he wrote the Honorable A. B. Beck, Circuit Judge of Lake Andes (family friend),

> Dear Judge,
>
> For some time, I have been undecided just what to do, whether to write to you or not. I thought I would try to secure a release without annoying you and others, but I understand that if I am to receive consideration from the parole board that it will be necessary for me to secure recommendations from the sentencing Judge and the prosecuting attorney.
>
> I realize that my appealing to you for a recommendation may place you in an embarrassing position, that you may feel that you should make such recommendation because you know my father. However, I am not asking you to favor me with such consideration unless you believe I am deserving and have earned this kindness.

All along I have contended, and I still hold to that opinion, that a man seeking clemency should stand on his own record, that outside influences should play no part in his securing consideration at the hands of the parole or pardon boards.

During the period of my incarceration I have stood steadfast in my determination to try to make amends for the wrong which I committed. During this time, I have tried faithfully to be of service to the officials of the institution by performing my work in a manner to merit their approval, and I am satisfied that every fair-minded official connected with the institution believes that I have played my part fairly and honestly.

I entered the institution October 13, 1933. I worked in the Rock Shed for 60 days then was transferred to the Twine Plant where I was given the job of shaking sisal --- a most dusty job --- I worked there for 30 days, or thereabouts, or until January 26, 1934, when I was transferred to the Print Shop. In June (the 14th), I was placed in charge of the Shop and have served in that capacity since that time.

We print all the forms used in the institution --- in the neighborhood of 200 forms as well as the little monthly magazine, *The Messenger*, which I believe you receive regularly.

My being in this place has caused my children untold embarrassment and humiliation. They were up to see me recently, and I trust that for their sakes at least, that I will be able to secure a parole and get out where I can start over again in some business or work which will not bring reproach upon them.

My daughter is 22-years-of-age. She is teaching school at Lohrville, Iowa (during the school year). This summer, however, she is the recreational director of Anderson Park in Sioux City, Iowa. She has held this latter job for two years previous to this year. She has taught school (the 5th grade) in Lohrville for two years past and was elected to teach the same grade the coming year.

My son is 17-years-of-age --- a fine young man. He is a junior in high school. It is needless to say, I am interested in his welfare.

At present, I have no parole sponsor but believe I will be able to secure one provided I can secure favorable recommendations from you and Mr. Halla.

One thing that is certain, I will not embarrass my father or relations by asking them to aid me in securing a parole signer, for I believe it is not fair to them.

I have not approached the officials of the institution relative to my securing clemency and their attitude toward such action, but I am confident that they would do nothing to hinder my receiving consideration at the hands of the parole board.

It is needless for me to state that I have regretted taking the steps which caused such havoc in every manner to my folks. I have had plenty of time for reflections, and I can assure you that my future conduct will be along safe and sane lines of honest endeavor.

I want to thank you, Judge, for your kind letter and Christmas greetings during the years I have been here. They have helped to cheer me a lot.

One thing I want to make clear is that if for any reason, you feel you cannot recommend me to the parole board for clemency, that I would like to learn this fact so can settle down to do the balance of my sentence.

> Thanking you in advance for a reply to this letter, I beg to remain,
>
> Sincerely and respectfully,
>
> Percy Kunkle

This well-crafted letter was Grandpa's first recorded effort to secure parole. He had served four years and eight months at that point for a theft of about $1,000. On that same day, he also wrote a letter to Mr. Halla, attorney-at-law from Tyndall,

> Dear Mr. Halla,
>
> I thought I would be able to secure consideration from the parole board without bothering or embarrassing people on the outside, but I am informed that is an impossibility. For that reason, I am writing to you to learn if you feel you can consistently recommend me to the parole board for clemency. I don't want to ask you to do anything which you believe is not to the best interests of society.

Grandpa again explained his work history in the prison culminating with his becoming the editor of *The Messenger* which he offered to send some copies to Mr. Halla. Grandpa continued,

> My record here is good, as I am confident the official record will state. I have never approached the Warden or Deputy Warden relative to their recommendations or in regard to my applying for clemency.
>
> I am not employing any angles to secure a release as many do, for I believe a man should receive clemency, if he is worthy of such consideration, not because of his political or other connections. I don't want to embarrass my folks in any manner to secure

clemency. They have suffered too much already because of my folly.

I am appealing to you as a man to man. If you cannot feel your way clear to send me a recommendation addressed to the parole board recommending clemency, then I surely don't want it.

During my time of incarceration, I have honestly tried to make amends for the wrong I committed. I have tried to promote the ideas and ideals which will tend to help the men incarcerated to become better men and to believe that a life of wrongdoing is contrary to everything which civilization has stood during the past and for which it stands today. I have tried to be of help to the officials of the institution in an honorable manner.

Regardless of what you may decide to do relative to recommending me for clemency I believe you will have done what you believe is right. That is what every man should do.

I do know that it is a sad mistake to keep a man incarcerated for years, releasing him only at the expiration of his sentence, for the chances he will become a charge of the State under such conditions. Every man serving time will be released some time and it is true that it would be to the advantage of the state to release a man under supervision for a period of probation before his sentence expires, rather than wait until he completes his sentence and is released without supervision or a chance to adjust himself to a new world. Mr. Halla, you have the check reign in your hands relative to my securing a recommendation from the prosecuting attorney, and I believe you will be fair to me and grant me a chance to get outside where I can do something of a nature which will enable me to provide for the time when I'll be unable to work.

I wish to assure you that I will not get into trouble in the future through any act of wrong-doing of my own, that I'll respect your faith in me by living as a law-abiding citizen should live.

Thanking you in advance for a reply to this letter, I beg to remain,

Sincerely and respectfully, Percy Kunkle[20]

Judge Beck responded three days later June 22, 1938,

Mr. Percy Kunkle, Sioux Falls, S. D.

Friend Kunkle:

I have your letter of June 19 and have read the same with a great deal of interest.

I have been thinking about you to a considerable extent lately. When I sentenced you, it was my thought that you should be released upon parole just as soon as you were eligible. I have spoken to your father about these two or three times and suggested that steps be taken to procure for you a parole. I also spoke to one or two members of the Yankton Bar about the matter. They all agreed that this course should be taken, but apparently, no one took enough interest in the matter to procure a parole guarantor and the necessary recommendations. I intended to write you about the matter but was waiting for the people at Yankton to take the initiative.

I shall be very glad to recommend that you be granted a parole at this time. I am sure Mr. Halla feels the same way about it. However, I shall talk that matter over with him the first time I see him. Whenever you are ready to proceed let me know, and I will prepare and submit the recommendation.

I have enjoyed reading your magazine very much. You are to be congratulated upon the excellent quality of your publication. I am sure you have mastered the printing trade; and you should be able to find suitable employment in that line without difficulty. In seeking a parole guarantor, you may use my name as a reference if that will help you any.

With kind, personal regards and trusting that you may be one of us again soon,

I am Sincerely yours,
A. B. Beck (Judge); Lake Andes, South Dakota
(Laura A. Pricket, Court Reporter)

Halla also responded to Grandpa's letter of the 19th on June 28, 1938,

Dear Percy,

Your letter of June 19, 1938 was received a short time ago, and let me say that I was very glad to hear from you. Your letter was very interesting and very well written. It did me good to think of the "heads-up" way in which it was written.

Before I forget it too, I wish to congratulate you upon the quick way in which you rose to the top in the work of the institution. I received the copies of *The Messenger* and although I have had time to look at only two copies, I will say that it is just a good little magazine. There is a big improvement in it over what it used to be. All in all, I am glad because of the good work you are doing and because your record is good.

I take it from your letter that you want a parole and not a pardon. If I am wrong in this, let me know. I have not looked up my code relative to any of this, for the past four or five years so am rusty relative to such matters. Therefore, I wish you would write me another letter giving me in brief the time your sentence would be over, whether or not by law you are eligible for what you seek – parole or pardon – and whether or not you have ever had any trouble with any of the powers that be at the institution. Also, let me know just to whom and where you want a letter or letters directed. Being close to such matters, you no doubt could tell me just how to proceed. John Daub and I talked matters over, and he too will be waiting until I hear from you.

Surely, I will be glad to do what I can, and on that you can depend. I might say that I also talked to Dennis (jeweler), now of Yankton, who was the fourth man in the car going up on October 13, 1933. If you think that a letter from him too would be of any use, I believe that I can get it for you easily. I shall await a reply.

Very truly yours,
Henry Halla.

On June 30, Judge Beck wrote to the Honorable Board of Charities and Corrections of the State of South Dakota, and his Excellency, the Governor of said State,

The undersigned, one of the judges of the First Judicial Circuit of South Dakota, and the judge who passed sentence in the case of State of South Dakota - vs- Percy Kunkle, determined in the Circuit Court of Bon Homme County, South Dakota, hereby respectfully recommends that the said Percy Kunkle be granted a parole at this time.

Mr. Kunkle was convicted, upon a plea of guilty, of Grand Larceny. He has now served more than half of his term. He was never in trouble before .... The writer knew him for years. Prior to the time he was sent to prison, he had an excellent reputation and was a good and upright citizen. I believe, if given his liberty at this time, Mr. Kunkle will take his place in society and become a useful member thereof.

Yours very truly,
A. B. Beck, Judge

Judge Beck then wrote Grandpa on June 30, 1938 to let him know he wrote a letter on his behalf recommending he be paroled. For some reason, though Grandpa was recommended for parole in June of 1938, eight months passed before anything was done. On February 26, Grandpa wrote Judge Beck another letter requesting parole. The judge wrote back that Grandpa could use his recommendation of the previous summer or, if he preferred, he could write a new recommendation for him. He went on to write,

> I have been wondering why you were not released on parole. In seeking a position and a parole guarantor you may use my name as a reference, and I shall be glad to give you a very good recommendation; and to assist you in every way possible. With kind, personal regards and all good wishes, I am,
>
> Sincerely yours,
> A. B. Beck (dated March 2, 1939)

By March 31 of that year, Grandpa finally found a parole guarantor, G. G. Laselle, who wrote to the honorable Norton Jameson of Sioux Falls, South Dakota,

> Dear Mr. Jameson,
>
> Am enclosing a Guaranty of Employment for Percy Kunkle, signed by myself and Judge Howard Babcock, of the fifth judicial circuit. The county judge here refuses to say that I am either respectable or responsible and very seriously objects to my assisting in any way any of the men in your institution. While on the other hand, Judge Babcock, approves of my feeble efforts to assist some of the boys. I am writing

you this as I have had to write every Warden for the past eight or ten years, so that you would know the reasons the county judge did not certify for me.

Yours sincerely,
G. G. Laselle

A form, "Guaranty of Employment" ... probably printed by Grandpa and the other three men in the print shop ... was signed by G. G. Lasalle, an attorney from Sisseton, South Dakota on March 31, 1939. On April 6, 1939, the warden of South Dakota Penitentiary wrote to the State Board of Charities and Corrections that he believed Grandpa had served his time. He must have met with Grandpa on April 5, 1939, for Mom wrote him a letter dated April 6, 1939,

> Dearest Daddy,
>
> Thank you for the letter. I'm so glad you accepted the Sisseton Attorney, as you say it'll give you an opportunity to get something better or work up there. Board and room is no small item either. I truly think it's fine. Last night was the night you were to have made an application. Hope it turned out for the best. Next Easter will be so different. I'm looking forward to it. Today, I'm sending Granddad a card. It's too bad that he had a stroke, but it's fortunate that his mind is OK, so often it isn't in a case like that.
>
> No exact word about election here. Wish they'd tell us - one way or the other. Mr. Lorenz talked to me about what he wanted me to do next year. But it's not down on paper and that's what I want.
>
> Typing class is over - last night. We each gave 50 cents and got him (the teacher, H. Hubbard) a scrap book, also a book end. Then had a surprise lunch - ice cream, cake, Ritz (crackers), mints, and coffee. He was really surprised and extra pleased.

Nothing from Sioux City yet. There's nothing quite like suspense I always say. Happy Easter.

Love, your daughter,
Edythe Louise Kunkle

Grandpa wrote his parole guarantor, attorney G. G. Laselle, on April 3. He had received a letter from Laselle on April 1 who wrote,

This certified that I am personally acquainted with G. G. Laselle Attorney at Law, who resides at Sisseton, South Dakota, who has signed a Guaranty of Employment for Percy Kunkle, a prisoner now serving a sentence in the South Dakota Penitentiary, and who is an applicant for parole before the State Board of Charities and Corrections and the Governor of said state; that believing the said G. G. Laselle to be a respectable and responsible person, and that he will employ him at fair remuneration as soon as paroled. We believe he will take a friendly interest in him and council and direct him in that which is good ...

Signed by the state attorney.

In July 11, 1939, Grandpa received a letter of support sent to Mrs. Grace S. Crill, Secretary of the Board of Charities and Corrections, Elk Point, South Dakota which read,

Dear Madam:

I am given to understand that the petition for parole of Percy Kunkle, comes up before the Board at the August meeting. I desire to take this opportunity to intercede in behalf of the petitioner. I was sheriff at the time that he got into difficulties with the law. Knowing the circumstance that led up to it and being acquainted with him personally, I'll venture to say that he is not a criminal character, by no means, and I believe, that if given this opportunity to be freed, he will make good. Will appreciate your kind cooperation in reporting favorably on the above application.

Sincerely,
John Daub, co-treasure of Bon Homme County, Tyndall, South Dakota.

Grandpa also received a supportive letter from the state attorney that convicted him, Henry Hall,

> Mrs. Grace S. Crill (dated July 8)
> Secretary, State board of Charities and Corrections
> Elk Point, South Dakota
>
> Dear Mrs. Crill:
>
> The purpose of this letter is to recommend to the Board of Parole that a parole be granted to the above-named Percy Kunkle as soon as such can be arranged. The writer, as State's attorney of Bon Homme County, South Dakota, had charge of the prosecution of this prisoner at the time of his conviction and commitment in October of 1933. When the matter of this parole comes before the Board for consideration, I take it that it will have before it a more or less complete history of the case so I am not touching on the same here.
>
> My understanding is that Percy Kunkle is eligible for parole in that he has served over half of his term of ten years, allowing time earned for good behavior. I understand too that his prison record is good and that he has made the most of his situation while there.
>
> Having fully in mind this prisoner's earlier life and background, the circumstances relating to and surrounding the crime for which he was committed to prison, his record as a prisoner and in general his

healthy attitude toward life, I would say that he has served a sufficient length of time and that his temporary release would be without danger to society. I consider that he has served long enough to pay his debt to society and firmly believe that the confidence placed in him in the form of a parole would in nowise be misplaced. He has taken his medicine like a man, and it doesn't seem to me that any purpose will be served by holding him any longer.

I strongly recommend that Percy Kunkle be granted a parole as soon as the proper arrangement can be made. Any information the board may desire, and which I am able to give regarding Mr. Kunkle, will be gladly given.

Very truly yours,
Henry Halla

To His Excellency Harlan J. Bushfield, the Governor; Pierre, South Dakota

SIR:

The foregoing recommendations, files, and records having been presented to the State Board of Charities and Corrections by the warden of the South Dakota Penitentiary, this board has made careful examination of all said files and records and made such other investigation as was necessary to determine the fitness of said prisoner for release on parole and, being satisfied, as a result of such investigation, that said prisoner may be temporarily released on parole.

We the undersigned, constituting the State Board of Charities and Corrections, recommend to your Excellency that said prisoner, Percy Kunkle, be paroled in accordance with the law of this State providing therefore. Done at Sioux Falls, South Dakota, this 6 day of April, 1939...

The governor responded,

Executive Chambers
Pierre, South Dakota

Be it known to all men by these presents: That I, Harlan J. Bushfield, Governor of the State of South Dakota, having carefully considered the foregoing recommendations and finding them sufficient, do hereby order that said prisoner, Percy Kunkle, be released from the Penitentiary at Sioux Falls, South Dakota, on parole and delivered to G. G. Laselle, Sisseton, South Dakota, in whose care he is to remain until the end of his term, or until, in the judgment of the Warden of the South Dakota Penitentiary or the State Board of Charities and Corrections, it may seem advisable to transfer the said prisoner to some other responsible employer, or until further order of the Executive of the State; said release to be granted immediately upon receipt of copy of this order by the Warden of the Penitentiary.

Executed at the Capitol in Pierre, South Dakota this 10 day of April, AD, 1939

Signed by the Governor and the Secretary of State.

Harlan Bushfield, Governor of South Dakota

Upon Grandpa's release, he moved to Sisseton, South Dakota where he submitted monthly parole reports. The first was dated April 30, 1939. Grandpa's first job was general laborer. His employer was G. G. Laselle who paid Grandpa $10/month. He apparently gave up using liquor and did not gamble or associate with unworthy people ... he signed the monthly parole reports accordingly. His wage was increased to $15/month with board and room in July of 1939. He shocked with a threshing team out of Sisseton for Oscar Rahlstad or Oscar Schaunaruan. He was paid 25 cents/hour in August ... $80/month. He threshed with Ole Iverson. Grandpa had the intestinal flu for one week in August. His address was Sisseton, South Dakota c/o Olaf Sjoberg. He had finished threshing with Alfred Iverson on Monday, September 4 and worked for Guy Tarvin as a house mover. He lived at 212 Second Avenue East Sisseton, South Dakota. Tarvin paid $150/month with board. He then worked for Hillman Rice at 30 cents/hour. He worked for Tarvin until noon on Nov. 27. He had no work for Grandpa 8½ days prior to that date. Hillman Rice was a former Mayor of Sisseton and a carpenter by trade and according to Grandpa, a highly responsible and respected man in the community. Grandpa found work with him and was paid 30 cents/hour.

Four questions were asked of Grandpa every month: "Do you abstain from intoxicating liquors"? "Do you frequent places where liquor is sold or drunk"? "Do you engage in any form of gambling"? "Do you avoid criminal, vicious, unworthy associates"? Grandpa replied "no" to "Do you avoid criminal, vicious, unworthy associates" in December and August of 1939. On the December 31, 1939 parole report, Grandpa answered the questions and signed the form, "P.S. Happy New Year Mr. Cole[21]! Thanks for your full-hearted support in my behalf during the year 1939." - Percy

Grandpa continued working for Rice at 30 cents an hour during January of 1940. He again said "No" to his monthly question, "Do you avoid criminal, vicious, unworthy associates?" Grandpa used his last monthly parole report form in February of 1940 and requested more. Grandpa still had no full-time job in March but was getting along OK. He made a trip to Wheaton, Minnesota to see about working on Lake Travers Project. Grandpa wrote in his monthly report,

> There will be quite a lot of work here this spring as soon as favorable weather arrives, and I am confident I'll be able to find something as I have a reputation as a good worker here - With best wishes and regards,
>
> Sincerely,
> Percy

In April, he indicated a possible building going up he might have found work with. In May, Grandpa was working for Haslew Contracting Company, Ortonville, Minnesota and Mr. Theilen of Sisseton at 30-40 cents/hour. Grandpa was working on the apartment house in May of 1940. That was the last parole report on file.

In talking with Joan Dare on June 12, 2013, she said some in the family looked down on Grandma for having gone through two divorces at a time when that was uncommon. The implication was she must be doing something wrong. I heard it from others myself. Nothing is further from the truth and hopefully this record, while honoring Grandpa's excellent qualities yet mindful of his humanity, seeks to vindicate Grandma's character and reputation as well. Mom said that Grandma was concerned some might think she was a recipient of the stolen funds, which she was not. Grandma's first marriage ended in her husband's infidelity as recorded in Part II, *The Dakotas.*

After Grandpa left Sisseton, the family lost contact with him. Mom was unable to locate him to invite him to her and Dad's wedding in June of 1941.

We know now that by 1945, Grandpa was a ship fitter[22] working in the Seattle shipyards. He lived in Poulsbo, Washington. His work ID number was 67-8817, and he was listed as being 5'10", 160#'s; 53 years-of-age with hazel eyes and black hair. He had a scare on his lower right cheek. Grandpa had an ID card dated February 23, 1960 and was still working at 69 years-of-age.

In 1945 he was living in the Territory of Hawaii working as a ship fitter. We're not sure how long he was based there before moving back to Seattle. He filed for divorce in 1946 to marry an Indian lady named Rita from Seattle. I assume he was back in the Seattle area at that time. Rita was an alcoholic, and the marriage did not work out.

When Grandpa's mother passed in 1953, Mom attended the funeral. I was with her as a newborn infant. In writing Great-Grandma Kunkle's obituary, Grandpa's sister Ruth, dropped his name from his mother's roster of children which, obviously, only served to hurt Grandpa and his children. Grandpa did not attend his mother's funeral.

After the funeral, Mom and Uncle Harry went to a restaurant and happened upon Birdie (Richard), Grandpa's brother. Mom asked if he was in contact with Grandpa, and if there was a way they could reach him. He said that he would let Grandpa know they were wondering. Shortly after that, Grandpa reconnected with Mom and the rest of the family.

I first met Grandpa in Yellow Stone Park. Dad asked me if I knew who he was. I said I did not. Dad said, "That's your grandpa" to which I replied, "My grandpa lives in Iowa." I picked up on Grandpa's habit of splashing cold water on your face every morning to wake up. Grandpa visited the farm when I was 10 or 11, but I don't remember his visit.

I was surprised by how many letters I received from Grandpa as a young boy. I'll include a few letters he sent to Mom and Dad as well. Here's one Mom sent to Grandpa:

Dearest Dad,

Must tell you what Tim said the other day. "You know our other Grandpa - I'm lonesome to see him." He has it in his mind that you live in a jungle where wild animals live, and you have to get there by a big boat (He has the zoo, the Canada trip and the beautiful foliage around your grounds all mixed together) - also Yellowstone, because he said how we fed the bears there too. Oh, my! I surely hate to have him go to school this fall - my baby. He is so dear. Mary will be in the 8th grade, Pat 6th, and Susie in 2nd. They're growing up ...

We went to Anthon - near Sioux City - yesterday for dinner at Clem's brother Leonard's (a vet and graduated from Ames in the same class with Harry). Their oldest boy came home with us for a couple weeks. He's 6-years-old. Wonder if he'll last two weeks. He had to sleep with Clem from 11 on last night. I finished off in the boy's bunk bed - so 5 this a.m. found me more sleepy than usual.

Clem's bro - a Dr. in Topeka, Kansas - bought a farm here this year and Clem is farming it too. They are to start building a new barn on the place today. They're to use a car load of cement.

Haven't all the house cleaning done. Still want to paint the dining room and kitchen, also finish the porches. I don't seem to be very speedy. I'll miss Mary the next two weeks. She and Pat and Sue weny two weeks to Bible school (all day!) Mary is real capable. Pat leaves next Sunday for a two-week camp trip in Kansas. Don't know how we can let him go. He's my right hand. We've been putting the chickens in the freezer. And you should see him catch and help dress the roosters. He gathers the eggs. Sue puts them in the egg case. Why Clem and I haven't a thing to do. No wonder we're fat and lazy!

Glen's came on Decoration Day. We all went to Harry and Iz's that evening. Harry and I really have a work out. Dr. Pomeroy is in the hospital – had his leg operated on, was kicked by a – something. This will be a bit early but want you to know all is well here and that we're hoping you have the best Father's Day ever.

Doesn't seem like 17 years for Clem and me on Wednesday. I had a wall desk made for Clem to be put in the kitchen. It's to be just for Clem! Farmers have loads of reports now days. Love, Us (Father's Day, 1958)

This letter was sent from Grandpa, to Mom:

Perhaps, that is why your great-great grandmother was about 105-years-old when she passed away. The last time I saw her, I was perhaps about ten years old – and she was keeping house for her son and a hired man on a farm near Rutland, Iowa. She seemed to be everywhere always on a trot it seemed. She baked her bread, cookies, cakes, made cheese, and took care of the chickens and geese. She was about 84-years-old when I was there! And Tim, so glad he enjoys the piano, music is a wonderful comfort and to have training broadens one's outlook. He will never regret the time spent in practice, I am sure. ... Glad you have gas heat – It's clean as you say – be sure the chimney doesn't choke up from coal dust soot and slacking lime etc. Perhaps you will recall, at Lead the priest who died from gas fumes due to a soot clogged chimney. (November 18, 1962; Poulsbo)

Grandpa wrote a letter on November 8, 1962 and spoke of Mom's gg-grandmother that lived to nearly 105 on a farm near Rutland, Iowa (Serena Ponsness, see page 188). He said he had last seen her when he was 10 and she was nearly 84 years-of-age. He referred to Mary's move to Washington,

It will be hard to give Mary Lou up but I am sure she has a wonderful mother who has given her high ideals and goals to work for. But she will find the good true and rewarding life through her own efforts. I am sure Mary Lou will make decisions in her daily life which will be a blessing to her and everyone she comes in contact.

Grandpa referred to each of us specifically,

On August 30, 1964, Grandpa wrote a letter to Mom and Dad from Poulsbo, Washington; Route 1; Box 374. He thanked them for the wonderful time he had had in Iowa and recounted his trip back to Poulsbo, visiting his brother Montrose, in Centerville and sister in Midland.

Grandpa also began writing me:

Dear Tim,

Just to let you know I do think of you so often. Bet you are a big help around the place and that you really do a good job with your school work too.

Love from Grandpa Kunkle, 1961

Dear Tim,

You must be growing up fast. So glad you are doing so well with your piano playing. Sort of have a feeling you are a regular guy – one who can do whatever must be done – and do it right. Hope you are all OK. It's looking better here – the sun was out most of the afternoon and I hope we have good weather balance of this week.

Love, Grandpa, June 27, 1963

Dear Tim,

I was so happy to hear from you - glad you won two blue ribbons out of your two exhibits. You Cavanaughs sure did all right at the flower show! Sorry you lost the last ball game, Tim - but, then, someone had to lose. If you did your best, you needn't feel too badly. Glad, Tim, you have a new car. It must be a grand thing to see. I am sure you will help to take good care of it. Mary made the best cake ever, Tim, and I must watch out or I'll become eligible to be the fat man in a side show! She also makes a wonderful banana bread as well as cooking everything so good! It would be nice to see you all, but a farmer must work at the job or lose out - and, of course, you don't want to lose. Hope you can help your mother and Dad. They need you and you need them. It's so good to work together. Mary misses you, Tim. She is always so happy to hear from you. Write whenever you can.

Love from Grandpa, August 4, 1963, Poulsbo, Washington

Dear Tim,

Trust your Easter is a happy time. You must be kept real busy with your school work and activities. So glad you are in the quartet. Have had such fine weather here - too dry though - had to water the flower beds. Hyacinths are in bloom. Some trees are blossomed out too. Weather is cool - shower predicted. Temperatures are to be below normal for next 5 days. Happy Easter, Tim.

Love, Grandpa

Dear Tim,

Just a line to let you know we are thinking of you and hope you are having a good time. How did you come out with the final ball game? Hope you won. It's real cool here - felt almost cool enough for frost this morning.

Love, Grandpa

Dear Grandson Tim,

Just to let you know I haven't forgotten you - as a matter of fact, no day passes that I fail to think of you. Glad you have a nice calf. I hope you receive a blue ribbon this year. I am sure you will do your best to win! How are you and all the rest of the family? Glad you are doing so well in your school work.

Love, Grandpa, April 11, 1965

Dear Grandson Tim,

It was so good to hear your voice over the wires on December 8. So happy you are doing good work in school - that your other activities are rewarding. I am sure you have abilities which will enable you to take an outstanding place in the world.

Love from Grandpa. (no date)

Grandson Tim,

Just to let you know I do think of you and wish you every happiness this Easter time and throughout the years to come.

Love, Grandpa ...

The card said, "May the love of our Savior bless you and keep you today and always." (Easter, 1967)

Dear Tim,

It is so nice to recall our being together last August -

thanks Tim for making my visit so pleasant. My hope is that you will always be as sincere and honest and straightforward and thoughtful of others as you were last August. Wish you the very best of everything, Tim.

Love from Grandpa (February 7, 1965)

Dearest Darling (to Mom),

Didn't know what to get you. If, for any reason (color, size, style, etc.) you can exchange it at a Sears store for some other item.

Lots of love and a Happy Birthday,
Dad

Grandpa sent a letter on March 8, 1964 where he mentioned how proud of the family he was and of Mary's plans to prepare a meal for the Zechs. He bought five rose bushes at Sears the previous Saturday and 96 Glad bulbs and Dahlias. He made one reference of me, "I am so glad that Tim likes his calf, and I have an idea that the calf is happy also."

Grandpa sent a letter to the family on April 25, 1964 from Poulsbo. He spoke of how well Mary Lou was doing. He mentioned he had just called her. He also had a letter from Montrose. He said, "Montrose said that there was neither bus nor passenger train service in Centerville now. Sure is different than when I was there. At that time, there were three passenger trains each way every day." He spoke of looking forward to driving to Iowa for an upcoming visit. Grandpa wrote again August 30, 1964, recounting his drive back to Seattle from his Iowa trip to visit us.

On May 14, 1967, Grandpa officially joined the Methodist church in Chehalis, pastored by Rev. H. C. Williams. Mom said he opened-up with the pastor on his prison years. He was embraced and well-respected by the church he attended and served. He lived at 512 Ohio. I had the opportunity of locating his home.

One of the final letters Grandpa wrote was to Sue on July 26,

1969. He wrote, "Darling, I pray for you every day. Oh, I do want you to find real joy and happiness in your life! ... God bless you, Susan, I am sure He has a very important place in life for you! Love, from Grandpa."

Mom and Uncle Harry went out to see Grandpa during his final days. Grandma offered to join them if she could be of help. Mom thought not. Mom contacted Dad to let him know that Grandpa didn't have long. Dad responded with this letter sent to Grandpa just days before his death, a letter which gives much insight into Dad,

> Dear Grandpa –
>
> Edythe called last night and told me of the seriousness of your illness and that you also know.
>
> I am sorry it must be this way. I am glad you were given time, by God, to prepare. I remember our first meeting, thirty years ago. You were living at Sisseton with a man and wife whose name I don't remember, but reminded me of Scattergood Baines[23], an old character in stories that use to be in the old *American Magazine*.
>
> The first time I saw you I liked what I saw. A stoic philosophy that would give strength to endure the endless injustices that seems to plague some people. I believe you were one of those ... On the second day of our marriage, Edythe and I spent it on the claim (Nowlin, South Dakota) with your mother. It would have been the sixth of June, but it was cold. I remember your mother wrapping herself with newspapers to keep warm.
>
> In her eyes, I saw the same stoicism and philosophy that I had seen in your eyes at Sisseton. She too lived a troubled life. I know, and so do your children, that some injustices dealt you, were not of your own making that you "took the rap" for someone not worthy to be in the same room with you.

All through the pages of history are told stories of people who endured wrongs of some kind or another. Whether it is geographical, environmental, or social, by parents, brothers and sisters, nieces, husbands, and children, by superiors, and by our fellowman. These lives are endured because of a philosophy strengthened by a grace from God.

My faith teaches that all men must do penance before going to heaven. Either here, on earth, or in the hereafter. I believe you have done yours, and when the time comes for you to meet our God, He will say, "Well done, my good and faithful servant."

I probably won't get to see you again, but I would like to thank you for your daughter, my wife for nearly thirty years, and I can truthfully say, I am glad you were my father-in-law.

Most sincerely,
Clem Cavanaugh

Grandpa died of pancreatic cancer in Seattle a few days after receiving Dad's letter. After Grandpa's estate was settled, he had $600 to his name. Coincidentally, the same amount Grandma Kunkle possessed after her estate was settled.

Mary was present at Grandpa's death, visiting him while living in California. Mom and Uncle Harry were there also. Mary was in Grandpa's room when he passed. After Grandpa died, Mom offered Mary $50 to buy a change of clothes for Grandpa's funeral. I haven't talked with Mary about this, but Mom thought Mary did not take the money, nor did she go to Grandpa's funeral.

In 1986, Julie, Erin, Caitlyn, and I flew to Seattle, Washington in route to see Dad's college graduation in Helena, Montana. After visiting the World's Fair in Vancouver, we drove across Washington to Helena stopping at Chehalis to see Grandpa's home and gravestone. We visited Gaffney relatives in Spokane. It was the first snow Erin and Caitlyn saw.

Mom says she never makes a bed unless she thinks of her dad. He was meticulous in the care of his belongings. I have a copy of Grandpa Kunkle's hymn book (page 96) which he signed while still living in Centerville, South Dakota, before moving to the homestead in Nowlin.

Percy Kunkle is in the back row with sister, Ruth, to his left. It is believed the other children are Percy and Ruth's Oakland cousins.

Percy Kunkle in Chehalis, Washington

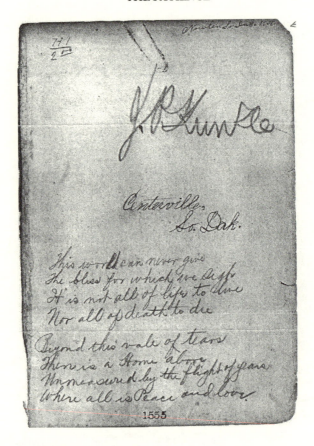

The poem he selected for its cover was:

> This world can never give
> The bliss for which we sigh
> It is not all of life to live
> Nor all of death to die
>
> Beyond this vale of tears
> There is a home above
> Unmeasured by the flight of years
> Where all is peace and love

Edythe Louise Cavanaugh (nee Kunkle); faithful daughter, faithful mother

The Kunkle homestead: The Diamond K Ranch

PART II

The Dakotas

Chapter 5

Ten Mile Country

Greene County serves as the southwest cornerstone of the State of Pennsylvania. It is home to the great Monongahela River called the Mon by locals. It meanders northward from Morgantown, West Virginia into downtown Pittsburgh, where joining with the Allegheny River, it becomes the Ohio and continues its southwestern journey to the Mississippi, providing the southern borders of Ohio, Indiana, Illinois, and the entire northern borders of West Virginia and Kentucky.

Ten Mile Creek ran perpendicularly from the west into the Monongahela River creating a bull's eye for early Mon River settlements including many of our relatives.

Prior to 1750, when the Kunkles were first arriving to the New World, French missionaries, trappers, and traders made their way into this great river valley and as early as 1771, white men began settling what had been the home of the Iroquois Confederacy consisting of Mohawks, Oneidas, Onondagas, Cayugas, Senecas, and the Tuscaroras Indian tribes. The Mon River Valley became a hotbed of immigration in the mid-eighteenth century with Britain, France, and the various Indian tribes laying claim to the area, a dispute settled by the French and Indian War.

Joining the Mon, midway between Pittsburgh and Morgantown and a few miles south of Interstate 70, a small creek, ten miles in length, zigzags perpendicularly and then "T's" into the north flowing Monongahela River becoming the bulls-eye of the Mon River Valley settlements. From the time of the French and Indian War (1756-1763) to the end of the eighteenth century, the tributaries of this Ten-Mile Creek would be inundated by pioneers, many of them German, British, Scotch Irish, Swiss, Dutch, some of them spillovers from the great migration into Kentucky[24], and others, travelers who passed through Baltimore in route to one of the great migration trails. Scores of forts were built as the frontier jumped over the Allegheny Mountains[25] into the Mon River Valley. Permanent settlements took root with the construction of these forts. The Jacksons, Shrivers, Kirkpatricks, Shulls, Ehrhards, Pattersons, and Keeners, all relatives of ours, were among the early settlers of Ten Mile Creek with the Kunkles not far away in Bushy Run and Irwin. These settlers cleared the land and farmed in close proximity to one another and to newly built forts.

Even with the forts, settlements among the Indians were very dangerous. **DAVID KEENER,** my 4-great grandfather, is a case-in-point. David's father, **UHLERICH KEENER,** left the Palatinate of West Germany and sailed from Rotterdam on September 27, 1727 on the *James Goodwill,* (twenty years before the *Patience* brought Johannes Kunkle to America). David Crockett was master. A relative told Grandma Kunkle that she and her mother both had the darker, Keener complexion as compared to the lighter Jackson complexion.

Uhlerich Keener settled in the Shenandoah Valley where he built his home until better lands lured him away in 1773 to Fayette County, Pennsylvania[26]. He purchased 300 acres in Fayette County and lived there until his death in 1784. Of his three sons, David made his home in the Ten Mile Creek area and became our ancestor.

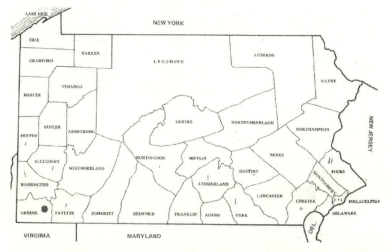

Greene County Pennsylvania was the location of the confluence of Ten Mile Creek and the Monongahela River. Many of our ancestors settled in this area.
Subsequent generations continued in the Westward Movement and became early settlers of southeast Ohio.

David was working his ground when the fort bell rang its warning. David's wife, children, friends, and neighbors made their way to the fort, bringing their livestock with them. David, however, did not hear the warning and continued working in his field. He was killed and scalped by these Indians, and vultures led family and friends to his body several days later. He left behind his wife, **HANNAH EARHART KEENER** and daughter Hannah who later married Henry Jackson Jr. **HENRY and HANNAH JACKSON** became my 3-great grandparents pictured on the next page.

Henry Jackson Jr. was born in 1770 and would die in 1838. He was the son of English immigrants, **HENRY JACKSON SR. and ELIZABETH STUMP** (born, 1745; April 4,1824), daughter of **THOMAS STUMP and JANE BOOTH**. Elizabeth Stump is buried in the old cemetery in Byesville, Ohio. Jane's father was **ROBERT BOOTH**. We don't know her mother's name.

> Before the Revolutionary War, they (Jacksons) lived on the site of what is now Washington D. C. when there was no city there. They lived near the "Poison

Fields" so called because a weed poisoned the noses of horses and cows. — *Kith & Kin, 244.*

Henry and Hannah had eight children. Their seventh daughter was my 2-great grandmother, **MARGARET ROXENA JACKSON**, who married **SAMUEL KIRKPATRICK**. Margaret and Samuel's sixth child, a boy, was killed at eighteen by a horse. He was my grandma Kunkle's great-uncle.

The Jackson family, under the leadership of their patriarch, Henry Jackson Jr., built Jackson Fort in Washington County near Fredericktown, Pennsylvania in 1759 (just as the Kunkle's moved to Bushy Run, nearly fifty miles away). Fifteen years later, in 1764, Henry, his father and sons built another fort which was inside the present limits of Waynesburg, Pennsylvania on the south bank of the south fork of Ten Mile Creek, no more than 10 miles from their previous fort. Ruins of this fort were extant as late as 1888. Daughters of the American Revolution have marked the site of Jackson Fort by a bronze marker on a street in Waynesburg.

Henry Jackson Jr., the builder of forts and Hannah (nee Keener)

Jackson's Fort in Ten Mile Creek began with a single cabin and later each additional family, wishing to take refuge in numbers, built their own cabins beside the others. These cabins formed a square and enclosed an acre or more of ground. Between the cabins were palisades 10 or 12 feet high. The doors of the cabins opened within the enclosure and the center area was a place of common usage. The outside of the cabins had neither windows nor doors. With forts constructed, land cleared, and the on-going movement of settlers and Indians to the West, families gradually established themselves securely in the valley. The cover of Howard L. Leckey's book, *Ten Mile Country and Its Pioneer Families*, depicts what Jackson Fort would have looked like.

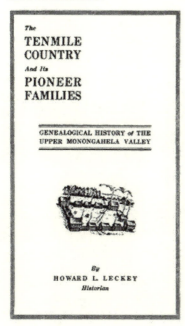

Grandma Kunkle and Great Grandma Kirkpatrick received a letter in 1912 from a Henry Jackson Dennison, a relative on the Jackson line. He was responding to a letter Grandma sent him requesting information on her Jackson ancestry. This letter was printed in *Our Kith and Kin*, Volume II, by Lorena Burke, page 6,

On my mother's father's side my great grandfather, Henry Jackson, before the Revolutionary War, lived near where Washington City, D. C. now is, when there was not a house there, and the place was called "The Poison Fields" as horses' heads or noses were, at times, made sore or poisoned by some kind of vegetation. He left the fort (where his family was for safety), going to his farm in winter, when an Indian sprang from behind a tree, aiming his gun at grandfather's breast; the gun missed fired and grandfather ran among the trees, the Indian firing at him but missed, and he returned to the fort. My great grandmother's father's name was Stump; and he was of English descent, and her mother's name before marriage, Booth, of English descent.

On my mother's side, my mother's grandmother's name before marriage was Airhart (this is an Anglicized Pennsylvania German form of Ehrhardt, Ehrhard, or Ehrhart) and after marriage, "Keener." Her husband, Keener, my great grandfather, was from Germany and his wife was of German descent.

Keener was shot by the Indians and ran and fell dead in his own wheat field during the Revolutionary War. My grandfather's (mother's father) name was Jackson; and he moved from Greene County, Pennsylvania to Guernsey County, Ohio in AD 1809; and my mother was born in Greene County, Pennsylvania. I, myself was born in the town of Mount or Point Pleasant, Ohio, January 6, 1842.

In a similar letter written to my great-grandma Shriver, Mr. Dennison wrote, in 1912,

> I suppose you know that my mother, at nine years old, went to live with her grandfather and grandmother, and consequently heard and knew more of relatives than your mother or any of her sisters ... This Henry Jackson, our great grandfather's wife's name before marriage was Booth. This goes back to the early settlement of America. Henry Jackson Sr. was of pure English blood; also his wife was of English descent. They had blue eyes; but the Keeners had dark eyes and hair. Your mother and Aunt Hannah Dillon were in complexion like the Keeners; my mother and Aunt Mary Woodrow had blue eyes like the Jacksons. Now Martha, you and your children, as well as myself and children, have Jackson, Keener, Airhart, Stump, and Booth blood in our veins.
>
> — Very Truly Yours, H. J. Dennison

In addition to the Keeners and Jacksons, a third family, the Shrivers (Grandma Kunkle's maiden name), made their home in Ten Mile Creek. **ADAM SHREIBER** was born in 1736. He was the first of the Shriver line to come to America from Germany prior to the Revolutionary War. He moved to Maryland then to Winchester, Virginia and during the Revolutionary War, was living in Frederick County, Virginia and married in 1758. Adam supplied 418 pounds of fine flour at 60 pounds per hundred-weight to Richard Eastin as food stock for the Colonial Army (Public Claim No. 86, Frederick County, Virginia). He was still living in Virginia in 1782 as the head of a household of 11. He moved to Dunkard Creek, Greene Township, Washington County in 1784 and was classified a foreign resident. On March 10, 1803, he and his wife, **CHRISTIANA STROSNIDER**, sold 180 acres of land on Dunkard Creek to their son, Abraham (Monongalia County DB 30 p. 4). Adam died and was buried on Dunkard Creek near Pentress, West Virginia where an illegible tombstone marks his grave to this day. His son and our ancestor, **JACOB SHRIVER** (from whom John Glenn descends), served as a body guard to General George Washington after the War.

Our ancestors on Mom's side were definitely part of the Westward Movement. After they first arrived to America, five successive generations would move westward in quest of inexpensive land: first to America's eastern seaboard, then crossing the Allegheny's to Ten Mile Creek, on into Ohio, Iowa, and eventually the Dakotas.

Adam and Christina Schreiber had five children[27]. Their son, Jacob Shriver, was born in 1759 and died in 1815. He was buried in Whiteley Township, Greene County, Pennsylvania nearly ten miles southwest of Ten Mile Creek but not before he and his wife, **ELIZABETH SHULL**, moved from Ten Mile Creek 75 miles westward into Guernsey County, Ohio. Elizabeth (Shull) was born in 1761 and died in 1803, the mother of ten. Jacob's second wife, Jane Mooney, was born in 1771 and died December 21, 1836. She and Jacob had three children. Jacob Shriver had a tract of land on the same fork of Big Whitely, a tributary of Ten Mile Creek, on which Henry Jackson Jr. lived accounting for the numerous intermarriages between the Jacksons and the Shrivers.

Jacob Shriver, though he would move to Ohio for a time, was buried in Pennsylvania which would always be home. But for his children, caught in the Westward Movement, Ohio became their home as they entered history becoming among southeastern Ohio's first settlers. Other Ten Mile Creek families joined the Shrivers in their migration into southeastern Ohio including the Kirkpatricks and Jacksons.

Chapter 6

Ohio

Henry Jackson Jr., the builder of forts and pioneer settler of Ten Mile Creek, moved to Ohio in 1809. He settled near Point Pleasant on what later was known as the Ebenezer Johnson farm situated ½ mile south of where the Pleasant City railroad station later stood. Except for one daughter, Polly, he temporarily left his wife and family in Pennsylvania to prepare for a move to Ohio. While in Ohio building a cabin and clearing land with Polly's help, his wife, Hannah (pictured on page 104), daughter of David Keener (scalped by Indians), died in childbirth in 1809. Henry returned to Pennsylvania, sold the farm, and moved to Ohio with his entire family. He would move from Point Pleasant to Jackson Township to a farm homesteaded by John Dixon whose deed was signed by President James Monroe. Henry latter married Rachel Tustin of Whiteley Township and raised another family. A common expression Henry was known for saying after a meal was, "Johnnie, while you rest, chop some stove wood."

The resemblance between Margaret and her grand-daughter, Grandma Kunkle's mother, was so similar, their old-age photos made them look like twins (page 104 and page 118).

Henry's oldest daughter, Polly, was helpful to him in preparing their Ohio home for the rest of the family who followed them into Ohio. Polly would later marry John Fish, whose family was the focus of *Our Kith and Kin* as related by Lorena Burke. Polly's obituary is included in the book,

> At the age of ten, she became a Christian and never after doubted her conversion. She became a member

of the Baptist church some years afterward and received the ordinance of baptism at the hands of Father Broom, a well-known minister of the Association, and ever after lived a devoted Christian life. For years past, her great age and failing physical powers caused her to desire to depart and be with Christ. She was tenderly cared for by her son John Fish until his removal west, then by her daughters Martha and Nancy in their homes. The sons and daughters providing every possible care for her comfort and well-being. - *Our Kith and Kin,* pg.110.

Henry and Hannah's daughters included Polly (married Henry Woodrow), Elizabeth (married John Fish); Ruth (married David Thompson); Nancy (married Elias Dennison); our relative, Margaret (married Samuel Kirkpatrick); and Hannah (married Vincent Dillon). Margaret Jackson[28] and Samuel Kirkpatrick's daughter, Martha Kirkpatrick married Michael Shriver's son William Shriver. William and Martha Kirkpatrick were my great-grandparents.

The Jackson family cemetery is in Byesville, Ohio. Henry Jackson Jr.'s stone states: "born 1770, died 1838, aged 68 years." Rachel Tustin Jackson, "born 1789, died 1871." Henry Jackson Jr.'s mother's tombstone is also there, "In Memory of Elizabeth Jackson, wife of Henry Jackson Sr., born in the year 1745, died April 4, 1824."

Jacob Shriver also left Ten Mile Creek and legend has it that he arrived in Ohio with two horses, leading a cow with Elizabeth holding their first baby on her lap. Old-timers used to point out the hollowed Sycamore tree on the stream that runs through the Frazille Stephens farm, which when cleaned out, furnished a snug haven for Jacob and his family until they erected their first cabin on the William Orndorff farm. Jacob purchased the tract of land on which he spent his first winter on March 9, 1786, under the title of "Jacob's Inheritance." These early, familial migrations into Guernsey County constituted the first settlements into southeastern Ohio, settlements made possible through hardships we'll never fully appreciate. My grandmother Kunkle knew this area well and in 1939, in route to the New York

Mary Kunkle (nee Shriver) at her parent's home in Ohio. Note the split rail fence that was in the farm yard.

City World's Fair with Uncle Glen, stopped in Ohio to visit many relatives and took pictures of some of the original Shriver lands.

Our Kith and Kin relates the day David Thompson and Ruth visited the Woodrows. Some in the community didn't like Thompson for how he treated Ruth. Being a Hard-Shelled Baptist, family worship was important to Henry (Ruth's father). Henry asked Thompson to pray. The family knelt in front of their chairs. Henry's sister, Nancy, leaned over and pinched Polly during the tiresome prayer. Thompson finished on the verge of everyone getting up to leave[29].

Michael and Jane Shriver's tombstone located in the Shriver cemetery near Dexter City, Ohio.

Nearly bisecting Wheeling, West Virginia and Zanesville, Ohio on Interstate 70 was Cambridge, Ohio. The Shrivers and Jacksons left Pennsylvania and settled a few miles south of Cambridge near Byesville, Ohio. In 1801, land was being sold for $2/acre in Byesville. Five of Jacob's ten children married one of Henry and Hannah Jackson's kids and two married

Patterson's[30]. Jacob's third child, Adam, had a daughter Jane, who married a White. Jane (Shriver) White's daughter, Mary White, married John Glenn I. Mary (White) Glenn was Grandma's second cousin and the mother of John H. Glenn II (Mom's third cousin). Grandma Kunkle's second cousin once removed, Mom's third cousin once removed, and my fourth cousin was John and Mary Glenn's son, astronaut John H. Glenn III[31].

Glenn came to the Tattered Cover Bookstore on November 12, 1999 to promote his book, *John Glenn: A Memoir*. While a United States Senator, I sent him a letter submitting the information I had that substantiated our sanguinity. He affirmed our connection on Senate letterhead. I took that letter and my family and went to the Tattered Cover to meet him. With a line of 800 people, we were turned away. I asked an attendant if he could show Glenn my letter, which he did. Glenn moved us to the front of the line and signed his Memoirs for me. We talked at length and had a photograph taken of the entire family with him and his wife.

Mr. and Mrs. John Glenn III at his book signing at the Tattered Cover Bookstore with Tim and Julie Cavanaugh family.

> **United States Senate**
> WASHINGTON, DC 20510
>
> December 20, 1989
>
> Reverend Tim Cavanaugh
> 8461 East 105th Avenue
> Henderson, Ohio 80640
>
> Dear Reverend Cavanaugh:
>
> You seem to have done a great job in the geneological research area. I have had a number of family trees sent to me in the past by different people following the orbital flight back in 1962 but they have certainly not gone into it in the kind of detail you have. I am not familiar with the Shriver connection in the background but your line-up of people must be correct for the Mary Glenn, John Glenn, John Herschel Glenn succession is certainly correct.
>
> You indicated that by my father's name you had the address, Shadyside Paris, New Concord, Ohio and that you were not sure what that meant. That part I can straighten out for my boyhood home was on Shadyside Terrace in New Concord, Ohio. The house was later moved to a new location when a road came through and took that particular lot off the map.
>
> In any event, from your research it would indicate that we are indeed fourth cousins.
>
> Best regards and hope you have a wonderful Christmas and the happiest of New Years!
>
> Sincerely,
>
> John Glenn
> United States Senator
>
> JG:dt

Jacob Shriver would return to his Pennsylvania home for burial but his son, Michael Shriver's home became the state of Ohio. **MICHAEL** was born in 1797 and married **SUSAN JOHNSON** in 1818. Susan was born in 1799. Michael Shriver's barn was 104 years old in 1939 and was still standing when Grandma visited. Grandma's journal entry reports, "The purloin timber which runs the length of the barn at the base and roof were 55 feet long, of oak, not spliced. The barn is near Dexter City, Ohio." The milk house had been moved twice but was in good condition. Grandma visited the Shriver cemetery on the old farm. It is surrounded with an iron fence. Michael died of heat stroke at 45 years-of-age while fighting a fire in an old tobacco house. Someone went on horseback through the woods to bring back a doctor from Zanesville, 40 miles away, but Michael died before the doctor arrived.

Left to Right: Elizabeth, Andrew, Martha, Elmer, William, and Jennie Shriver.

William and Martha Shriver's farm site they left to move to Iowa. The brick house was torn down and sold for chimneys.

Michael and Susan's children were Jacob (1819-1904), Sarah (1822)/John Steen, Adam (1825-1847), Nicholas (1824-1907), Michael (1827-1919)/Mary Hughes, Joseph (1834-1878), Amanda, William (my mother's grandfather), John, Susan, and Elizabeth. Michael and William ("Billy") both were rumored to imbibe to excess and both moved westward into Iowa for affordable land.

Michael and Susan's son, **WILLIAM SHRIVER**, married another Ten Mile Creek/SE Ohio immigrant family's daughter of Irish descent, **MARTHA KIRKPATRICK** (my grandmother Kunkle's parents). Martha told Grandma Kunkle that they were related to Andrew Jackson although we've not confirmed that. I can say the Kirkpatricks and Andrew Jackson's family both immigrated from Northern Ireland (a relatively small area) about the same time, so it is certainly possible. In any case, it was for that reason, William and Martha named their first-born son, Andrew Jackson Shriver, whom Mom and Uncle Harry respected greatly.

Great Grandpa William Shriver inherited 34 acres and the home place when his father, Michael, died in 1841. It appears that 25 years later, William and Martha had married and had two children before moving to Iowa on March 3, 1866. Grandma Kunkle learned the exact date they left Ohio from the trip she made in route to the New York City World's Fair in 1939. On that trip, she and Uncle Glen stopped at Hallie Shriver Hughes' home for a visit. Hallie's husband's journal entry mentioned that on March 2, 1866, Grandma's father and mother, William and Martha Shriver, sold their farm where Fulton and

Glen and Grandma Kunkle at her grandfather's barn in Dexter, Ohio in 1939 in route to World's Fair. Ray and Hallie Fulton are pictured with Grandma and lived there at that time. Michael Shriver built the barn in 1834.

Hallie now live. "It was a stormy day. The next day they moved to Belle Plaine, Iowa[32]."

Andrew, William and Martha's oldest child, was born in Ohio on May 9, 1862. Their second child, Elmer, was also born in Ohio in 1864. In other words, Grandma's oldest two brothers (Mom's uncles) were born during the Civil War! Martha was three months pregnant when they moved to Iowa and gave birth to their third child, Jennie, on September 15, 1866. Elizabeth was born August 29, 1875. Jennie or Eunice Jane died at the age of 11 on December 9, 1877 in Belle Plaine and is buried there.

Jennie or Eunice Jane and sister Elizabeth. Jennie died December 9, 1877 in Belle Plaine, Iowa.

I'm not sure if he rented, owned, or where he lived from 1866 until 1878 (Elizabeth was born in Persia, Iowa in 1876), but we do know he purchased their farm in Belle Plaine on October 10, 1878. William's farm situated at the East ½ of Southeast Quarter of Section 26, Township 78, North Range 42. William Shriver paid $640 for the property.

We know he bought land on January 2, 1882 in Harrison County (north of Omaha or just above Pottawatomie County, near Persia, Iowa) on January 2, 1882[33]. We know, however, his residence remained Belle Plaine at the time of that purchase. Grandma was born in 1881 and grew up in Belle Plaine on the Shriver farm until her father's death in 1892. William had a severe case of diabetes which ultimately took his life. I have wondered if William purchased the farm for his son, Elmer, who lived and farmed in the Neola/Persia area but am not sure.

William died on January 29, 1892 and was buried in the beautiful and unusual Oak Hill Cemetery in Belle Plaine, Iowa. Martha would move to South Dakota with her daughter, Mary (Grandma Kunkle) and homesteaded a section next to Grandma's. She returned to Belle Plaine after a few years where she passed and was buried.

Three Kirkpatrick sisters. Their children are pictured on page 120. Left to Right: Martha (6 kids); Hannah (husband was General Joseph Davis, 9 kids); Lizzie Kirkpatrick (married Nicholson, 9 kids).

William Shriver, Grandmother Kunkle's father

Martha Shriver, Grandma Kunkle's mother.

Chapter 7

Belle Plaine

Belle Plaine was one of the largest towns in the State of Iowa when the Shrivers moved there. The Chicago Northwestern Railroad built a round-house at Belle Plaine and decided it would be their regional hub. The transcontinental road, Highway 30 or the Lincoln Highway, was built through Belle Plaine in the 1920's. Little wonder so many relatives moved there, many to work the railroad. Ray Shriver and Andrew Shriver, Grandma's cousin and brother respectively, worked for the Chicago Northwestern Railroad based in Belle Plaine and John Bachman, Grandma's first husband, would make his way to Belle Plaine to work for the railroad.

After William's death and the farm sold, the Shrivers moved into this home in Belle Plaine.

In 1886, the town drilled a well that spouted water 53 feet into the air causing what is now known as the "Jumbo Well." It took 14 months to harness the world famous well. Grandma was five-years-old and still living on the farm when the well blew.

The Shrivers lived on their farm for 25 years before William died in 1892. My grandma, **MARY SHRIVER**, was 10 when he passed and one year later she and her mother left the farm and moved into a home located at 54 North Beech which was on the NE corner of 5th Avenue East in Belle Plaine. Mom and I located the corner lot their home was on but the house is now gone. Grandma would later homestead with her mother in South Dakota where she met and married my grandfather, Percy Kunkle whose family is covered in Part I of *The Patience*.

"Mary Nicholson, Mary Shrive Chase Davis - 3 friends" ~ Grandma Kunkle 1902

Three first cousins in 1902. Their mothers are pictured on page 117.

At about 5:30 p.m. on July 28, 1894, Robert Liddle, a blacksmith, was working at his forge repairing an iron wagon wheel. Grandma was 13-years-old and lived blocks away. The wheel had to be red hot in order for him to shape it and the sparks flew as he wielded the hammer. Loose hay was being delivered for the horses in order to have enough feed in the stable for any quartered there. A stray spark from the blacksmith's forge flew into the dry hay as it was being hoisted. The fire spread with the hot, strong July wind. Within 3 hours, 27 buildings were destroyed, effecting 80 businesses in town. Two of the first buildings to be burned down were City Hall and the fire department which destroyed some of the equipment needed to fight the fire. Sally Wertheim, the mayor and the owner of a clothing store made telephone calls to Cedar Rapids, Blairstown, and Tama for help. The Chicago Northwestern organized special trains to transport the equipment and men needed from these cities to fight the fire. As so often is the case, I wish I had asked Grandma her recollection of this incredible event. Her home was just blocks from the downtown area.

Grandma soon became a member of the Baptist Church in Belle Plaine and her commitment to her faith in Christ was central to her for the rest of her life. The First Baptist Church of Belle Plaine was organized on April 28, 1977 with eight people. The church building was erected in 1878 at No. 30 South Beech Street, the SE corner of Jefferson. It cost $2,500 and the membership sky rocketed from 8 to 152 at the time of construction. Reverend H. A. Brown was the pastor from 1891 until 1894, C. H. Moore in 1894, and J. E. Treloar from 1894-1897. Grandma would have remembered all three of these men. I have a copy of the original church biographical directory of 1897. The historians[34] at the Belle Plaine museum drooled over it. They have a copy but not the original. Grandma worked at a general store and was a telephone operator in Belle Plaine as pictured below (Grandma is the second from the right).

Jumbo Well, Belle Plaine, Iowa

Chapter 8

Bachmans

One employee of the Chicago Northwestern Railroad at Belle Plaine was a young man by the name of John Bachman. Bachman came from Bethlehem, Pennsylvania, a son of a Moravian bishop of Arlington, Pennsylvania. His mother passed at the age of 92 on March 7, 1932. The family had two sons, John and Joe, and a daughter, Mary, who married Charles Rietz.

The Moravian church is one of the oldest Protestant denominations in the world dating back to the Bohemian Reformation (modern day Czech Republic) which together with the Waldensians and the Lollards are among the precursors to the Protestant Reformation of Europe

H. E. Bachman, John's Father

led by Martin Luther in the sixteenth century. The Moravians' roots go back to John Hus who pressed for the liturgy to be in his native language, Czech; wanted lay people to receive communion of bread and wine; priests to marry; the elimination of indulgences; and the discontinuation of the concept of Purgatory. Hus was declared a heretic for these beliefs and was burned at the stake on July 6, 1415.

The Moravians were very active in missions in the early British Colonial period converting many Mohican people to Christ. John

142 S. Main Street, Bethlehem, Pa.

John H. Bachman

Wesley writes in his autobiography, *Strangely Warmed*, that it was the Moravians' faith during a great storm at sea on his return to Great Britain from the American colony of Georgia that helped him recognize his need for salvation. He later said he experienced his heart "strangely warmed" by their confidence in the face of death.

Count Zinzendorf led a small community of Moravians in a mission effort into Pennsylvania in 1741. The mission was established on Christmas Eve and called, "Bethlehem." Their missionary focus was to the Algonquian Indians. The motto of the Moravian Church was and remains, "In essentials, unity; in nonessentials, liberty; and in all things, love."

The highest order of ministry within the Moravian church is bishop, the office H. E. Bachman held. He would have been chosen by a Provincial Synod. His duties were not administrative but pastoral,

especially pastoring the pastors. Grandma Kunkle's husband, John, certainly was raised within a strong, Christian heritage. As a young man, he left Pennsylvania having acquired a job with the Union Pacific Railroad and moved to Belle Plaine, Iowa, a railway center for the Union Pacific.

We're not sure how Grandma and John Bachman met, perhaps at church or at the post office where Grandma worked. In any case, a romance developed and the 19-year-old Mary Shriver and John Bachman married in 1902.

John Bachman and Mary Shriver's wedding on June 4, 1902

Since transportation was free (John worked for the railroad), John Bachman and Grandma traveled to San Francisco for their honeymoon. Glen remembers Grandma telling stories of going to Catalina Island in a glass bottom boat and to Chinatown in San Francisco. I've seen a picture of Grandma on top of Pikes Peak in Colorado with a group of railroad employees. For a woman who never secured a driver's license, she got around in those early years!

The Union Pacific Railroad established a station and post office at Wilkens, Wyoming on April 21, 1903. John H. Bachman became its postmaster. It later discontinued on September 15, 1908 with its mail then being handled by the Green River post office. Wilkens was in Sweetwater County and had a population of 25 people.

Union Pacific Railroad showing location of Wilkins, Wyoming

Forty-four years prior to the Wilkens post office opening, regions of the US fought for the first transcontinental track, but when the South succeeded, Lincoln signed the Railroad Act of 1862 which gave the Union Pacific the right to sell Federal land in Laramie, Wyoming. 400 lots sold quickly and Laramie became a town. Until the railroad, Wyoming basically didn't exist!

From Laramie, the Union Pacific worked its way toward Promontory Summit, Utah Territory in the months ahead. It laid track through Wilkens and on through Green River. A specially-chosen Chinese and Irish crew had taken only 12 hours to lay the final 10 miles of track in time for the celebration to commemorate the historic event which was held on May 10, 1869 (34 years before Grandma and John Bachman opened the Wilken's post office). The Central Pacific's *Jupiter* came from the west and met the Union Pacific's No. 119. The two locomotives drew up, face-to-face, at Promontory Point where the last spike was driven to complete the Transcontinental Railway. Interstate 80 follows this line today.

Wilken's Peak, a small mountain (about 8,000 feet) in Sweetwater County was very near to Wilkens and pictured below. Just west of Wilkens, on the Union Pacific Railway line, was the Shale Cut also pictured below. The Shale Cut gives some idea how great an achievement it was to complete the Transcontinental Railway.

Shale Cut, West of Wilkins, Wyo. On line of Union Pacific
Postcard Date unknown
Published by Barkalow Bros. Omaha, Neb.

Grandma (nee Kirkpatrick) Shriver at a neighbor's in Wilkens, Wyoming

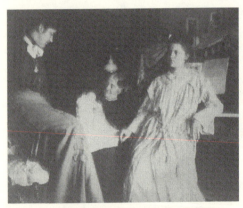

Gertrude Shriver, Great-Grandma Shriver with Glen, and Mary Bachman in their Belle Plaine home in 1905.

Ross was born in 1903 and in 1905, Grandma returned to Iowa for Glen's birth. During her absence, Bachman was unfaithful and subsequently acquired a sexually transmitted disease. Grandma, wanting to protect the children, decided to divorce Mr. Bachman.

Years later, during a visit at Uncle Glen's with Mom, Uncle Glen gave me a personal letter his father had sent him. It was written from Los Angeles, California and dated "November, 1934". Bachman expressed his pride for his boys and his remorse over his youthful indiscretions he dated back to 1905. He wrote,

> I left Nevada October 22, after getting my affairs settled there as there was no use of my staying in that cold country if the SP would not let me work, and it is so much cheaper living here, besides being close to my brother Edwin at Orange. He is 72 and in a bad way and health too. I am inclosing two tracts, which were once my father's and sent me by sister Mary which may be interesting to you.

The Rietz's left this past week for Florida and when they return in Spring, I expect to make my home with them at Salem if God is willing. By the way I feel now, I don't know. Having to quit working is bad enough but being sick besides is worse and all alone in the world too but as the Bible says, "The wages of sin is death" (Romans 6:23), and I can only wait for it. Being so unhappy, life does not hold much for me now. I have paid the penalty. My eyes were indeed blinded 29 years ago (1905), and I took all my blessings for granted. I attend meetings nearly every night and on Sundays to try and get some comfort, but I am afraid it's too late in life.

Glen Bachman and Tim Cavanaugh

When I go up there I will try and see you if still able to get around. Suppose you will be in St. Charles. Let me know. I left a good bicycle at Moor, Nevada which I used to go to work and for exercise. Wish there was a way for Harry to get it. I'll see about it in spring. Also, an oil stove and mill etc. I do not think they will OK me for work when I go to the hospital for an exam 1 of January, 1935 and too, that's in the dead of winter in Nevada.

You say your mother has three to support? I was under the impression she had only two children or does that include herself? Ross showed me their pictures when I was over there. Edythe and Harry's doctor gave me digitalis to take today for my heart. Besides, I have to inject 20 units of insulin before meals for diabetes of which disease your Grandpa Shriver died. Too bad they had no remedy then. However, it does not cure, only offsets the sugar in the food one must eat to live, and I have to diet besides - no cake, pie, or sweet foods - protein and fat food only is allowed.

Hard rains here last two days and nights - gloomy weather. I have no photos of myself taken lately, but if you want an old one, I'll send one. Have snaps of myself and Ross but guess you saw them. I have no mill here so excuse this pencil and paper.

You made a fine record at DWU and I am proud of you and of being your father however being so unworthy. Heard from Ross Nov. 1 and he was busy getting settled at housekeeping; I presume in his cottage on the beach. Must quit and go to church now, 11 a.m. Am enclosing two snaps taken in Kauai in January, 1893. If you have not seen them but maybe you have. You can get some idea of me. Am poorer in flesh now though.

Well, let me hear from you soon as you have time. I'll be here a few weeks yet. As ever —

Sincerely, Your Dad

Bachman died of a heart attack in 1936 in Nevada and was buried there. He had diabetes and was on a very strict diet. Ross kept in close communication with Bachman and, according to Mom, Glen to a lesser degree.

Uncle Glen said he always felt somewhat responsible for his father and mother's divorce since his birth caused their separation when Grandma returned to Belle Plaine for his delivery. Of course, that's not true, but sometimes, what makes perfect intellectual sense, doesn't always address our souls.

Joe & John Bachman, Brothers
About 1927

Divorce was uncommon in those days and there could be a tendency to cast dispersion on Grandma who was divorced twice. I believe Grandma Kunkle made the right choice under the circumstances foisted upon her to divorce Bachman. She should be vindicated and admired for the difficult decision she made to become a single mother. Her second marriage with my grandfather ended similarly, but under unique circumstances which I gave an account of in Part I.

Bachman never supported Grandma financially in either spousal or child support. Despite that, Grandma was not bitter toward him (or toward Grandpa Kunkle). I never heard any dispersion from Grandma toward anyone. It's sad to see the remorse and guilt John Bachman lived under and could only wish he had found the forgiveness I'm sure Grandma felt toward him, but more importantly, the forgiveness God extended to him through Christ.

Ross and Glen, October 1914

In my quiet-time yesterday, I was reminded of Isaiah's account of how Israel suffered the consequences of serfdom in Babylon as a result of their unfaithfulness to God. Isaiah recorded how they, as a nation, struggled with internal regret and believed that God had rightly hidden Himself from them due to their sin. God revealed to Isaiah (40:27-31) that just the opposite was the case. He understood their emotional struggle as revealed to Isaiah, "Why do you say, O Jacob, and speak, O Israel: My way is hidden from the Lord, and my just claim is passed over by my God"? God comforted them with these words (Isaiah 40:29-31):

> He gives power to the weak (to those who have blown it), and to those who have no might (slaves in Babylonian exile), He increases strength. Even the youths shall faint and be weary (the best among us share our humanity), and the young men shall utterly fall (even the gravest moral lapse committed), but those who wait on the Lord (set God and His promises before them) shall renew their strength (shall lift their heads high); they shall mount up with wings like eagles (they will go on with their lives full of

faith, hope, and love), they shall run and not be weary, they shall walk and not faint.

Salvation is not only the meaning of the name, Isaiah, it is also the theme of the Book of Isaiah, the book from which Handel drew most of his lyrics for his great composition, *Messiah*. It underscores that despite our sin, God still loves us and longs to redeem us. We learn from books like Isaiah and Galatians that our salvation and our relationship with God are based upon grace not our merit or good works. The first verse shared with me from Scripture said the same, "For by grace you are saved through faith and that not of yourselves, it is a gift of God; not by works, so no one can boast."

– Ephesians 2:8-10

After their divorce, Grandma returned to her family in Belle Plaine and lived with her mother for a year or two. She and her mother then decided to embark upon a great adventure. They became homesteaders in South Dakota.

Chapter 9

The Homestead

A series of laws, the Homestead Acts, gave applicants ownership of the land at little or no cost. The first of the acts was signed into law by President Lincoln in 1862. During the Civil War, the northern states wanted to encourage individual ownership of land as opposed to the southern model of slave owners using groups of slaves to their economic advantage. Later, during reconstruction after the Civil War, the Southern Homestead Act of 1866 was instituted. The Enlarged Homestead Act of 1909 increased the number of acres for a homestead to 320 acres for farmers accepting more marginal lands not easily irrigated because much of the prime low-lying alluvial land along rivers had already been taken.

Ross, Mary (Shriver) Bachman, Martha Shriver, Glen Bachman

The railroads took advantage of the Homestead Act to encourage settlements along their lines. On December 10, 1906, the long-awaited train, albeit a work train, first went through Midland, South Dakota. The workers continued to build the line west towards Philip and eventually to Rapid City. The depot and section house were erected and on April 7, 1907 at 2:00 p.m., the first regular passenger train pulled into the Midland depot with 123 passengers onboard. This was the end of the line for the passenger train, and the settlers disembarked and were soon on their way by stage or hired rig to their various claims or inland towns. Some settlers came in "immigrant cars" which were box cars loaded with possessions, possibly some livestock and the families themselves. At the end of the line they would unload the team and wagon and other belongings and travel to their claim. Others came in the passenger cars with a few possessions in the baggage car. The railroad was laid into Nowlin in the winter of 1906-1907 to a point two miles west of the Rifenberg Ranch. The following May, the rail was resumed and ultimately reached Rapid City on August 15, 1907 (*Historic Midland 1890-1986*). The last conductor on the last passenger train was Bunk Matthews. This train passed through Midland October 24, 1960. Julie Talledge and Roy Logan, who came in on the first train in 1907, were also on board.

For several years after Grandma's first marriage ended in 1905, she struggled to determine how to support her family in Belle Plaine. Being from a railroad community, she heard the railroad was promoting settlements near upstart towns like Nowlin, South Dakota which sprang up along their rail lines. It was an opportunity for Grandma to get ahead in life. She became a single-woman homesteader, a demographic constituting 10% of all South Dakota homesteaders.

Grandma arrived in Nowlin in early 1909, Great Grandma in 1910. They probably moved to town in 1911. Grandma married in 1914. Great Grandma most likely returned to Iowa in 1912 or 1913 (Glen would have been 7 or 8). When Grandma's mother left, Grandma wrote her sister, Susan Beam of Luzerne, Iowa. This note was on the back of the post card shown below,

> My Dear Sister,
>
> Your good letter does me so much good. I have been nearly sick since mother left. We are so glad our dear Saddie will be with us soon. Don't overdo dearest for

we all need all our strength now – Don't we? Glen was not to be on this picture, but he is. Dear heart, I am so sad. Love me so I can feel it through this gloom. Love to each from all.

Your Mary

Grandma's goal was to homestead 160 acres and she applied, according to Glen, at the Manila Land Office[35] in South Dakota. The application fee was under $20 and a small fee was paid as a commission to the land agent. She was granted a parcel of land near Manila, South Dakota. Another nearby settlement town was Ottumwa, South Dakota. Both Manila and Ottumwa were named after Iowa towns since so many settlers moved there from those towns. With her receipt in hand, Grandma made plans to build a home on the property and to make improvements on the property. Some properties required a five-year residency, South Dakota required a one-year residency. After the year was up, two acquaintances were required to sign a paper testifying that Grandma did live on the property in her own home for one year and made improvements on the property. This document was called the proof document which is where the phrase, "proving up" comes from. The homesteader who "proved up" had met the requirements to own the land. The Homestead Acts remained in effect until 1976 with provisions for homesteading in Alaska continuing until 1986.

The Nowlin Land Office opened in March of 1907. An announcement was issued that David Moore, United States Commissioner, had an office in the bank where, once a month, he would hear proofs and receive filings that were ready to come before the Land Office.

Grandma's Patent Record #39 is on file in Pierre. It was signed by President Taft on June 24, 1909 and filed August 1, 1909 at 10:30 a.m. as posted on Page 198 of Book 39. The land description is as follows: "Southeast Quarter of Section 35 in Township Five, North of Range Twenty-Three, East of the Black Hills Meridian, South Dakota."

Six months after Grandma filed, Grandma Shriver decided to support her daughter and returned to Nowlin and filed her own claim on 160 acres adjoining Grandma's. They built a home straddling the two claims thereby fulfilling the requirement that they each build and live in a home on their claim for one year.

Grandma Shriver's land was the "SW Quarter of Section 35 in Township Five, North of Range Twenty-Three East of the Black Hills Meridian, South Dakota containing one hundred sixty acres." Grandma Shriver's claim was also signed by President Taft. Grandma's land description was the same as Grandma Shriver's except Grandma's would have begun with "SE Quarter of Section 35 in Township Five."

Grandma was 29 and Great Grandma Shriver was nearing 68 when they moved to South Dakota with Ross and Glen. According to the book, *Land of the Burnt Thigh*, 10% of all homesteaders in Western South Dakota were single women. Grandma and her mother were leaving the "beautiful plain" (Belle Plaine) for the Great Plains which were void of trees except near rivers and filled with cacti and rattle snakes. Little wonder Uncle Ross decided to move to Hawai'i. But, as Mom would comment, "Most homesteaders were hopeful and positive adventurers. The smallest cloud would bring hope for rain, and they welcomed this opportunity." And so, in this way, my grandmother and great-grandmother stepped into the pages of history

PATENT RECORD NO. 39.

The United States of America.

Certificate No.

To All to Whom These Presents Shall Come, Greeting:

WHEREAS, Mary Bachman has deposited in the General Land Office of the United States a Certificate of the Register of the Land Office at Pierre, South Dakota, whereby it appears that full payment has been made by the said Mary Bachman according to the provisions of the Act of Congress of the 24th of April, 1820, entitled "An Act making further provisions for the sale of the Public Lands," and the acts supplemental thereto, for the Southeast quarter of section thirty-five in township five north of Range twenty-three east of the Black Hills Meridian, South Dakota, containing one hundred sixty acres,

according to the Official Plat of the Survey of the said Land, returned to the General Land Office by the Surveyor General, which said Tract has been purchased by the said Mary Bachman.

NOW, KNOW YE, That the United States of America, in consideration of the premises, and in conformity with the several acts of Congress in such case made and provided, have given and granted, and by these presents do give and grant, unto the said Mary Bachman and to her heirs, the said tract above described; TO HAVE AND TO HOLD the same, together with all the rights, privileges, immunities and appurtenances, of whatsoever nature, thereunto belonging, unto the said Mary Bachman and to her heirs and assigns forever; subject to any vested and accrued water rights for mining, agricultural, manufacturing, or other purposes, and rights to ditches and reservoirs used in connection with such water rights, as may be recognized and acknowledged by the local customs, laws and decisions of courts, and also subject to the right of a proprietor of a vein, or lode, to extract and remove his ore therefrom, should the same be found to penetrate or intersect the premises hereby granted as provided by law; and there is reserved from the lands hereby granted, a right of way thereon for ditches or canals constructed by the authority of the United States.

IN TESTIMONY WHEREOF, I, William H. Taft, President of the United States of America, have caused these Letters to be made Patent, and the Seal of the General Land Office to be hereunto affixed.

GIVEN under my hand, at the City of Washington, the twenty-fourth day of June, in the year of our Lord one thousand nine hundred and nine, and of the Independence of the United States the one hundred and thirty-third.

By the President: Wm. H. Taft
By M. H. Young, Secretary.

H. H. Sanford, Recorder of the General Land Office.

Recorded Miscellaneous, South Dakota, Vol.
Patent No. 67374

STATE OF SOUTH DAKOTA, County of Stanley.
Filed for record this ___ day of ___ A. D. 1909 at 10:15 o'clock A.M. Recorded in Book 39, Patent Record, on Page 198.

J. W. McKillip, Register of Deeds.
By A. H. McKillip, Deputy.

Mary (Shriver) Bachman's Claim

PATENT RECORD NO. 44

The United States of America

Pierre 17264   Certificate No. _____

To All to Whom These Presents Shall Come, Greeting:

WHEREAS, Martha Shriver

has deposited in the General Land Office of the United States a Certificate of the Register of the Land Office at Pierre, South Dakota, whereby it appears that full payment has been made by the said Martha Shriver according to the provisions of the Act of Congress of the 24th of April, 1820, entitled "An Act making further provision for the sale of the Public Lands," and the acts supplemental thereto, for the southwest quarter of Section thirty five in Township five north of Range twenty three east of the Black Hills Meridian, South Dakota containing one hundred sixty acres

according to the Official Plat of the Survey of the said Land, returned to the General Land Office by the Surveyor General, which said Tract has been purchased by the said Martha Shriver

NOW, KNOW YE, That the United States of America, in consideration of the premises, and in conformity with the several acts of Congress in such case made and provided, have given and granted, and by these presents do give and grant, unto the said Martha Shriver and to her heirs, the said tract above described; TO HAVE AND TO HOLD the same, together with all the rights, privileges, immunities and appurtenances, of whatsoever nature, thereunto belonging, unto the said Martha Shriver and to her heirs and assigns forever; subject to any vested and accrued water rights for mining, agricultural, manufacturing, or other purposes, and rights to ditches and reservoirs used in connection with such water rights, as may be recognized and acknowledged by the local customs, laws and decisions of courts, and also subject to the right of a proprietor of a vein, or lode, to extract and remove his ore therefrom, should the same be found to penetrate or intersect the premises hereby granted as provided by law; and there is reserved from the lands hereby granted, a right of way thereon for ditches or canals constructed by the authority of the United States.

IN TESTIMONY WHEREOF, I, William H. Taft, President of the United States of America, have caused these Letters to be made Patent, and the Seal of the General Land Office to be hereunto affixed.

GIVEN under my hand, at the City of Washington, the fourteenth day of February, in the year of our Lord one thousand nine hundred and ten and of the Independence of the United States the one hundred and thirty fourth.

By the President: Wm H Taft
By M.W. Young, Secretary
H.W. Sanford, Recorder of the General Land Office.

Patent No. 111107

STATE OF SOUTH DAKOTA, County of Stanley.
Filed for record this 2 day of April A.D. 1910, at 8 o'clock A.M. Recorded in Book 44 Patent Record, on Page 299

J.A. McKelly, Register of Deeds
By D.S. Williams, Deputy

Margaret (Kirkpatrick) Shriver's Claim

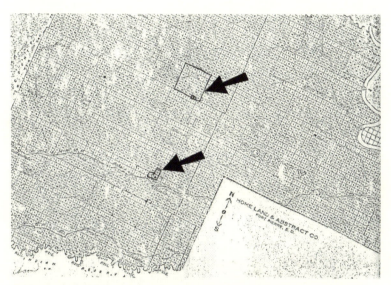

Grandmothers' Mary Shriver and Martha Shriver claims (two sections in bottom right of larger square above) in contrast to Grandpa Kunkle's father's Diamond K Ranch below. Both ranches were in Stanley County, South Dakota. The Diamond K was near the Bad River and just outside of Nowlin. The Shriver Claims were many miles from the nearest town of Nowlin.

by becoming one of the early pioneer settlers of Western South Dakota, for our family, the Westward Movement came to an end. The Calla Lillie in great-grandmother's right hand (page 143), her left arm was paralyzed by a stroke, speaks volumes of the character of these women.

Haakin County, home of Nowlin, South Dakota

Grandma Shriver

It's not known whether they rented or owned their home in Belle Plaine. I understand that after William Shriver's death, the bills were far more than anyone realized and there wasn't any money left. William was only 55 when he passed which may, in part, explain their financial challenges. Perhaps they rented and were motivated to homestead in order to own their own property.

Grandma left Belle Plaine and took her piano with her. She also took a flat-topped trunk which Mom gave me. Mom said she would take naps on top of the trunk. Most people came to the new country with no transportation and no idea of how to find their land. C. D. Joy engaged in the land business and came to Midland in 1906. He was a surveyor and showed available land to prospective homesteaders and located their claims for them. He also dealt in land and kept track of those who wished to give up their claims after a year or two. This was called a relinquishment. Usually the party who took over paid the original settler an agreed sum of money and a commission to the land man. However, the country filled up fast and in 1909 the land locating business came to an end. Grandma and her mother lived in a one room, tar-paper shack until the land was proved up. Uncle Ross said they lived initially in a sod home. Grandma wrote a letter to Susan Beem of Luzerne dated 1909,

Grandma Shriver holding a Calla Lillie. She had a paralyzed left arm due to a stroke.

Dear Aunt and All,

Here we are at last. Just going to build a house. Can we build yours next?

Lovingly, Ross and Glen.

As a high schooler, I asked Grandma if I could put her memories on audio tape. She was reluctant, but I began to ask her questions having subtly turned the recorder on. She recounted several memories, but how I wish I took greater advantage of that interview and had kept that tape! Grandma related how prairie fires were feared.

On one occasion, with an approaching fire, Grandma plowed around her tar-paper shack to create a fire-proof buffer of sod. Glen recalled Grandma mentioning a ridge of ground near the house diverted the fire.

She related going into Nowlin to purchase supplies (nearly 20 miles away). It was a full-day's effort. As she was going down the road, a large rattle snake was shaking its tail in the middle of the road. Grandma began to throw objects at it. Finally, a man approached Grandma from the opposite direction on the road, path really. Grandma explained her dilemma. He said there was nothing to worry about because she had broken the snake's back. The snake was summarily killed and Grandma was free to pass with the horse-drawn lumber wagon safely. Grandma had a set of snake rattlers I use to gawk at. I wonder if they were from that snake.

Glen, "Spicer", and Ross

Grandma also told the story of drawing water at her claim. She had to travel some distance, draw the water, and then filter it through towels. There was a reddish crustacean which left the towels red after filtering. The water would then be boiled and stored in a hole in the ground. In time, a shallow well would be dug. With so little water the same bath water was used by the whole family. After bathing, the water was used again to scrub the floors. Some of the shacks had dirt floors. The roads were grass and dirt. Mom shared that, "One time when

Mother went to get supplies such as sugar, matches, flour, and kerosene for the lamps ... the kerosene can sprang a leak and ruined the other supplies."

Behind Grandma's claim, a hole 5' x 5' was dug and a small building was placed over it. This would serve as the outhouse. Old catalogues left on the toilet seat were used for toilet paper. Mom related, "There was no electricity in these little huts. In the summer, Mother dug a 2' deep hole and put a crock jar in it. She placed butter and milk into the crock and covered it with a lid to keep the contents cool. Vegetables and fruit were canned."

Indians would travel from Cheyenne to Pine Ridge and passed by the claim outside of Nowlin. Mom remembers the Indian entourage passing by dragging their travois behind the horses with dogs feebly following. They sometimes stopped at the Kunkle ranch where Great-Grandma Kunkle (nee Oakland) gave them food. Grandma remembers them stopping at her grocery in Nowlin. Mom said Grandma sometimes feared Mom could be taken.

Winters were severe. Their heating stove could burn wood and coal, but they could not keep it burning all night. In the morning, the house was frigid before the stove was started. Mom continued, "Mother put eggs in a jar and put them in bed to keep them from freezing." Grandma cleaned the chimney on their kerosene lamp daily.

1, Glen; 2, Ross; 3, Grandma; 4, Spicer (the dog) in Nowlin, South Dakota

During the winter, ice was cut from water holes in the river where deep water froze a foot or more of clear ice or from water in dams near town. About January, crews of men with long "ice saws" and block markers (to guide the saw cuts in making uniform blocks), and horse-drawn sleighs or wagons "put up" ice. This was used to make ice cream, cool beverages, and cool the insulated wooden refrigerators in the summer. The ice was stored in tall frame buildings or in underground ice houses and packed in straw or sawdust.

Many of these activities were not just because they were homesteading, similar conditions were existing on the farm in Iowa. Electricity didn't reach rural Iowa, for example, until the late 1940's.

Mom continued,

> Summers were hot, windy, and dry. The land was fertile but with lack of rain, row crops were discouraged. In 1912 South Dakota had an extended drought and many homesteaders gave up and moved back to where they came from. Grass had nutrients that were great for livestock. There were few fences so the cattle were branded. Each rancher had his or her own brand. Mother's brand was "BS" for "Bachman Shriver," a source of some joking.

Life was certainly difficult. Glen remembered Grandma expressing appreciation for her many Iowa friends who all chipped in to help one another. Glen also recalled a covered-wagon tour of the Badlands being organized by the church but Grandma not going. Otherwise, there wasn't a lot of social activity except through the Methodist or Catholic churches.

Livestock was sold in Midland to A. E. Benedict in 1908. Henry and Bud O'Neil were hog buyers, as was J. W. Harry, "Happy Harry." They would buy cattle and held them at the stockyards until they had a carload, then shipped them out by rail. The bank was run by Ed Coshun. Pete Jacobson was the livery man. He once locked up Grandma's straying cow and fined her to get it out. Does anyone not have such a personality in their neighborhood? Charley Marden ran the store and Ed Scidler was the depot agent. Elizabeth Ries helped part-time in Grandma's home. The pastor, Everett Jarmen, took over Grandma's store when she moved to Lead. He was so opposed to liquor and tobacco he wouldn't sell them. Jarmen helped Ross and Glen get into college (Methodist college). Grandma wanted him to help with her funeral but outlived him. At one time, there was a bank, hotel, community building, and two general stores in Nowlin.

When they proved up, our grandparents sold their land and bought a grocery store and home in Nowlin with, according to Glen, the $1000 they got from the claim making the land's value at the time they sold at $3.125 per acre. The store had a post office in it. Indians came by often and, as Grandma related, often stole produce.

Pictured outside of Grandma's store in the picture below are several friends and family. The Jacobson boys played with Ross and Glen. Stanley well remembered them. The community of people in the photo are listed below.

1, Lonsdale; 2, Percy Kunkle; 3, Edward Jacobson; 4, Harry Bradley, 5, Mrs. Lonsdale; 6, Hazel Dillon; 7 E. Jarmin; 8, Bernice Jarmin; 9, Mrs. Jacobson; 10, Grandma Shriver; 11Mrs. Batty; 12, Mrs. Marden; 13, Grandma Kunkle; 14, Miss Spooner; 15, Mrs. Jarman; 16, Mrs. Morris and Baby; 17, Jerry Jarman; 18, ? Marden; 198, Montrose Kunkle; 20, Ross Bachman; 21, Nowlin Jacobson; 22, Stanley Jacobson (Mom and I met him, and he gave me a photo of his father's sod home), 23, Glen Bachman; 24, Teddy Marden; 25, Edward Batty; 26 Grace Marden.

Edythe Louise Kunkle (Cavanaugh)

Uncle Glen's account described the Nowlin house as having two rooms downstairs, a kitchen/dining room and a parlor with Grandma's piano. Mom was born in the parlor. There was one large room upstairs divided by a chimney and curtain. Glen remembers lying in his bed upstairs and hearing Mom crying after her birth in the downstairs' parlor. Glen wrote this poem to Mom, "Dear little sister of mine; how well now today I recall; those sweat curly locks of thine; that shone like the gold leaves of fall."

Mom was born one year after her parent's marriage on December 8, 1915. She recalls,

> I was born at home on December 8, 1915. My dad's father had a law office in Nowlin and also in Yankton, South Dakota at that time. My dear little Norwegian Grandmother Kunkle stayed in their homestead with their family. My grandpa Kunkle would keep the law business going and frequently came to the ranch. My dad and mother and Mom's mother were devoted Christians. The obstacles that the homesteaders encountered were enormous and were surmounted with dignity, faith, and hard work. I'm proud of my heritage.

Mom was named Edith Louise but went by her middle name Louise. As she approached her teen years, she decided to go by her first name, Edith. She later changed the spelling of Edith to Edythe, thinking it looked a little fancier. I asked Mom what Grandma thought of her changing her name from Louise to Edythe and Mom simply said, "Tim, I hope you're as patient with your kids as my Mom was with me."

A miscarriage would occur between Mom and Harry's birth which played a role in Grandpa and Grandma deciding to go to a hospital in Rapid City to give birth to Harry.

Grandma, (eventually Grandpa), Great-Grandma, Ross, Glen, and Mom lived in the Nowlin house together. It was crowded especially when Grandpa brought a newborn or sick calf into the house. Glen said Grandma worked in the general store and Great-Grandma helped with the kids and house.

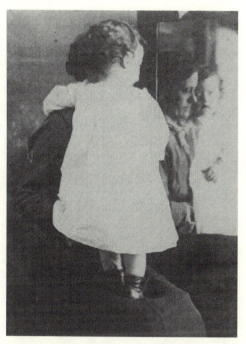

"Little Louise" on her mother's lap

He described his grandmother as,

> A buxom Irish lady with a good wit and very superstitious. If a fire did not burn, for example, she was sure someone was dying and sometimes they were! Dreams all were meaningful, and she had a dream book she used in interpreting them.

Glen said that she was a psychic of sorts. Once when he and Ross were going to a party, she became upset and began to cry fearing she would never see them again. They assured her they'd be back and did indeed return that night. The next day, however, they returned to Wessington Springs for school and never saw her again.

The school teacher at the little school in Nowlin was Percy Kunkle. Like Grandma Kunkle, he too was a homesteader in charge of his father's homestead while his father practiced law in Eastern South Dakota. He had a beautiful voice and played the violin at all the local gatherings and at church where Grandma played the piano.

Edythe Kunkle and her brother, Harry, playing behind the Percy House on the Kunkle Ranch about 1922.

The book, *Circuit Riders of the Middle Border States* records, "In Stanley and Haakon counties the first circuit rider to visit the early settlers was John Wood." By 1907, the Methodist church circuit riders had five classes organized in Stanley and Haakan counties with a total membership of 160 people. Grandma became a Methodist in Nowlin and the church was an important part of my grandparent's lives. A romance soon followed and Grandma and Grandpa were married in 1914, Ross was 11 and Glen was 9.

Glen recalled the day Grandma told Ross and him of her plans to marry the young, local farmer, Percy Kunkle. Glen said it was OK but remembers Ross objecting.

According to Glen, they had a religious home with Bible readings and prayer at meals and at night before they went to bed. Grandma dipped into their meager earnings, Glen recalled, and bought a Scofield Reference Bible in December of 1921 for herself, Glen, and Ross with their names inscribed on it. I still have Grandma's. "Nowlin, S. D." was also inscribed on the cover. Grandpa loved to sing and though soft spoken, sang out very loudly. Bill Kunkle said that Grandpa was the tallest and most handsome of the Kunkles.

Edythe Louise Kunkle

Glen recalled the family making periodic trips to Iowa to visit relatives which included trips to Rinard to visit Mattie and Andrew. They also visited Uncle John Beem and Aunt Susie in Luzerne; Elizabeth and Bert in Ida Grove; and Elmer in Neola. Uncle Bert was a card, Mom said. She remembers him walking into the living room wearing Aunt Lizzie's nightgown, just for a few laughs.

The Teton River ran through Nowlin but because of its notorious tendency to flood was renamed the Bad River. Ross and Glen caught a fish in the Bad River and proudly presented it to their Grandma Shriver who prepared it for supper as a surprise for Grandma when she returned home from errands. Everett Gobel, as Glen remembers, was the town bully and Herman Ries came to Ross and Glen's rescue one day. His mother helped Grandma at her home.

The photo above was outside the rural home Grandpa lived in before marrying Grandma. It was called "Percy's Place." Taylor was found shot in this home.

> From left to right: Mrs. Heltzel ("Whitie"), Great-Grandma Shriver before returning to Iowa in 1921), Mary Kunkle (Grandma), Edythe Louise (Mom), Mrs. Staley. Perhaps Grandpa and Grandma moved here for free rent, having lived in a home in Nowlin at the time of Mom's birth.

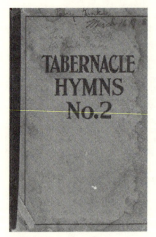

Uncle Glen said he and Ross crossed a train truss with Uncle Taylor. Russ and Glen made it across but Taylor wasn't going to. Taylor was about to jump when he crawled under the tracks and hung on to the support until the train surged by. Glen also remembered Grandma whipping him with a harness tug when needed.

Percy Kunkle's hymn book dated March 16, 1925; Lead, South Dakota.

On January 7, 1927, the South Dakota legislature formally invited President Coolidge to South Dakota for the upcoming summer. In the days before air conditioning, he liked cooler summer locations than D. C. offered. He decided to set up the 1927 Summer White House at the State Game Lodge at Custer National Park. He brought his pet racoon, Rebecca, and two collies: Robb Roy and Prudence Prim. While there, he attended the dedication of Mount Rushmore.

(As an aside, when Gutzon Borglum visited Mom's grade school, Mom helped finance Mount Rushmore by donating ten cents!)

President Coolidge front and center with Mom, the girl fifth to the right of Coolidge in a blue tinted dress, during the summer of 1927. Grandma, Grandpa, and Harry just below the right-side yard light.

This photograph shows attendees to a Methodist church conference in Rapid City, South Dakota. Grandpa and Grandma took Mom and Harry to this conference. The week before, a severe storm went through Rapid City and blew out a number of windows. President Calvin Coolidge is pictured front and center. Edythe Cavanaugh is in a slightly bluish-tinted dress, five people to the right of Coolidge and holding the hand of a young, unidentified child.

Grandma and Grandpa Kunkle are holding Harry Kunkle in the back row just below the yard light on the right side.

Education was very important to Grandma, so when Ross and Glen finished with country school in eighth grade and since there was no high school close by, she sent them to Wessington Springs, South Dakota to a Methodist boarding school for their high school years. Mom recalls how excited everyone was when they visited from school. Ross graduated in three years, then went to Dakota Wesleyan University where he majored in chemistry. His first teaching job was at Elbon, South Dakota about 20 miles from Nowlin. Glen rode his horse to visit Ross once and spent the night.

Since Ross and Glen went to Dakota Wesleyan to college, they were gone much of Mom's growing up years. Grandpa Kunkle was the only father they knew. Mom knew that Glen especially had a great respect for Grandpa.

Glen recalls Grandpa moving the family into their rural house or "Percy's Place," about eight miles outside of Nowlin. He tried to build a barn into the side of a hill using logs he cut from a large cottonwood tree. He ended up building a framed barn. Glen said Grandpa later sold that place to the Peterson's. Glen recalls Grandpa as being somewhat impractical. After selling to the Peterson's, Grandpa moved to the Meyer place next to the Kunkles. I think they ultimately lived in the Percy Place or the tar-paper shack on the Kunkle homestead a mile from the Pennsylvania Dutch style home that Great Grandma Kunkle lived in, and it was from that home they moved from when they eventually moved to Lead. Their first, temporary home, in Lead was at 12 Park Dale.

Glen and Ross enjoyed their pet dog, Spicer. Babe and Bright

Eyes were pet lambs. Glen rode a buckskin horse named Buck and Ross rode Ned who, one day, broke Ross's leg rubbing him up against a fence post, something my horse always tried to do to me. They threw a mattress into a lumber wagon and took Ross to Dr. Minard in Midland to set his leg. Ross also acquired a compound fractured wrist on a fall from Ned. Grandpa rode Brownie, a bay like Ned. When Brownie gave birth to a colt but couldn't nurse it, Ross was asked to put the colt down, according to Glen.

Glen later would teach at the Pleasant View Country School in Nowlin and recalled what a joy it was to teach Mom in her 3rd and 5th grades. Pleasant View Country School was about five miles from the Percy Place. Glen moved in with Grandpa and Grandma Kunkle and taught at the school. Mom remembers Glen driving her to school;

The first house in Nowlin, South Dakota. Peter Jacobson standing outside with a duck on a line. I met his son, Stanley, while visiting Midland with Mom. Stanley well remembered the Bachman boys and gave me this photo.

taking the kids to Pierre, South Dakota to see the capital; and drawing fish on the blackboard with math problems inside the fish to help the kids learn their math. Grandpa taught Mom in first grade and, after she came down with the croup, again in second grade. The country school Mom went to was walking distance from Percy's Place though Glen did have a car by then.

On March 23, 1924, Mom wrote Uncle Glen,

> I spoes that you are wondren if I would rit you. I was so bisse with my school work that I could not rit you sooner. Do you remember when you was out here that the ould bridge north of town, it was ? ... now this year they are making an new bridge. May have driven ten piling sin it all ready. Mrs. Toman is the cook for

the gang of men. I will rit a verse fore you, You say this to the cows on some night. Mooley cow, moley cow, come from the woods! They sent me to fetch you as fast as I could. The usn has gone down, it is time to go home, mooey cow, moey cow, why do you roam? Right soon,

your sister, Louise Kunkle, Nowlin.

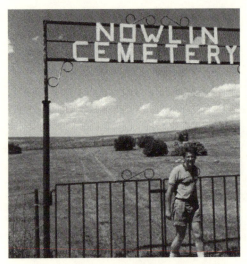

Tim Cavanaugh on a trip with his mom to Nowlin. The Nowlin cemetery was established on land donated by Great-Grandpa Harry Kunkle.

Times were very difficult financially for Grandpa and Grandma and ranching didn't produce much in those areas. Grandpa got his teaching certificate and began to teach third grade. Ultimately, Grandpa found work at the Homestead Goldmine in Lead. Grandma got up at 2:00 a.m. to make potatoes chips for sale the next morning at local outlets that Mom would take the potato chips to. Grandpa tried cosmetic sales for a time and finally left Lead to work as a bill collector for his father's law practice in Yankton, South Dakota.

Grandpa's sister and her husband, Ruth and Ray Noble, moved to Nowlin from Centerville and Grandpa's father, Harry Kunkle, wanted them to take over the ranch. Mom remembers Grandpa signing over the cattle to his father. Harry Kunkle practiced law in Yankton at that time but had a law office in Nowlin he purchased from Peter Jacobson and Ellen Jacobson for fifty dollars in October of 1909. It was located on Lot Six of Block One in Nowlin.

I took Mom back to Nowlin, South Dakota when I was home visiting from Gainesville. Ray and Ruth's gas station, vacant and abandoned, was one of the few buildings still standing there. Bill Kunkle wrote of his uncle and aunt's garage in an article entitled, "Little Garage on the Prairie" (11/19/2009),

> When US Highway 14 was a gravel road, the Ray E. Noble garage was new and a place where folks could get just about anything fixed or built. One farmer had a tractor made from a Model A Ford car. And his wife, Ruth, ran a roadside café called "The Squaw Cooler."

I climbed a large hill just to the side of the Bad River to get a bird's eye view of the area. In a chance encounter, we stopped at the senior center in Midland and Stanley Jacobson was there. He gave me a photograph of his father, Peter Jacobson, in front of their sod home, the first home in Nowlin. Mr. Jacobson was named after Stanley County.

Grandpa secured a job working for the Homestead Gold Mine in Lead, South Dakota and made plans to move. The homesteading life for both Grandpa and Grandma was about to come to an end. After he secured work, Grandpa wrote back and notified Grandma to bring the kids to Lead. Mom was 11 years old and Uncle Harry 6 when, on July 19, 1926, the community handed out invitations to promote a going-away party for the Percy Kunkle family. "Farewell Party for Percy Kunkle and Family; July 19 (1926) at Community Hall; Ice Cream and Cake; Everybody come!" I still have a copy of this invitation (pictured on page 158).

Grandpa Kunkle, third from right, on a hill in Lead, South Dakota.

Girl Scouts with Edythe Kunkle front row far right.

Though Grandma tried to spruce-up Grandpa's lunch bucket, still he dreaded the descent into the bowels of the earth. He sold cosmetics door-to-door for a while before moving to Yankton to work for his father in collecting bad debts. Mom recalls boxes of Walker cosmetics at their home in Lead, products Glen and Ross sold one summer. After a short time, Grandpa and Grandma moved from 12 Park Dale to 803 Searl Street where they stayed until they left Lead.

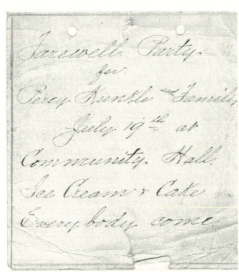

A community-wide invitation to a farewell party for the Percy Kunkle family as they prepared to move to Lead, South Dakota.

While in Lead, Grandma's store, which she was renting to Pastor Jarmen, burnt down in Nowlin. At that point, their rent money was gone and additionally, she invested her insurance money with an investment company which had gone broke despite their slogan, "No losses to investors in 50 years." Grandmother had nothing to show for her homesteading years.

Grandpa ultimately secured work with his

father as a collection agent in Yankton and moved there to support the family while they stayed in Lead. While apart, Grandma received a letter from her brother, Andrew Shriver, who lived in Rinard, Iowa. He found out that there was a post office job available that she should apply for. Grandma contacted Grandpa who wrote Grandma back and agreed she should take the job since collections weren't producing much income for him.

Grandma's grocery store burning down after she and Grandpa moved to Lead.

Grandma, Mom, and Harry took the train from Lead and passed through Nowlin in route to Iowa. Grandma had arranged for Harry to stay with his Grandma Kunkle on her ranch until she could get settled in Iowa. Harry got off the train and was met by Ruth and Lillie at the station. Mom vividly remembers Uncle Harry getting off the train but being told by Ruth and Lillie it wouldn't work out for him to stay with his grandma. The train was already shoving off as Uncle Harry desperately ran to catch-up-to and jump back on for Iowa. It was hurtful to both Mom and Harry. Mom said Lilly later apologized to Grandma for that.

The train stopped at Ida Grove and the family spent time at Lizzie and Bert Dillon's (pictured at their home in Ida Grove), Grandma's very supportive sister. Mom and Harry remained in Ida Grove for a few days while Lizzie drove Grandma to Rinard, the next chapter of Grandma's life story was about to begin.

Lilly and Bert Dillon; Ida Grove, Iowa.

Mary Kunkle, Edythe Louise, and Aunt Lillie at Kunkle well and water tank on their homestead in South Dakota.

Taylor Kunkle; Harry Kunkle; and father, Percy, at 802 Searle Street; Lead, South Dakota

Chapter 10

Rinard

Settlers first appeared in Rinard in the mid-1800's. The first men to register land in Cedar Township were J. C. Tullis (Mom knew the name) and David Young in 1858. They were the only settlers until the 1870's when Rinard experienced its first and only boom. The town soon grew and thrived around the railroad. My great uncle, Andrew Shriver, Grandma's brother, was the station agent and pictured below behind the depot in 1926 with his prized Jerseys. He grew livestock in a small pen attached to the rear of the depot where Uncle Harry remembered going to play as a kid. At its peak, eight passenger trains and several freight trains stopped daily at the depot in Rinard.

Rinard was founded in 1904 and incorporated the year Grandma and Grandpa married, 1914. 26 petitioned the district court on September 28, 1914 to be incorporated. A vote was taken and the "yes" votes won, 22-14. At one time, Rinard had a post office, hotel, restaurant, hardware store, blacksmith shop, barber shop, meat market, drug store, cement block and tile factory, two real estate agents, two

Andrew Jackson (AJ) Shriver, Grandma's brother, with his favorite Guernsey cows behind the railroad station he worked at as the station agent in Rinard, Iowa.

grain dealers, two churches, a gas station, bank, library, grocery store, and two railroads.

AJ's son, Ray Shriver, was an agent for Chicago and Great Western Railroad. Mr. Fisher ran the grocery store. I remember going there as a child and buying candy. Mom would sometimes ask Grandma if she needed anything in Fort Dodge but Grandma preferred paying more at Fisher's to help him stay in business. Andrew's daughter, Mary Martha Shriver, whom we called Aunt Mattie, also lived in Rinard with her husband, Fred. They ran the hardware store. We were all proud of Grandma Kunkle for starting the library in Rinard and, of course, she was the postmistress. Our Shriver family were a big part of Rinard's early history.

Grandma moved to Rinard because her brother, Uncle Andrew, who was born in 1862, learned that the post office job was available and contacted Grandma who was living in Lead, South Dakota at the time. It would be a temporary job lasting months to a year with the possibility, but not the guarantee, that she could become the postmistress. Grandma wrote Grandpa, who was living in Yankton at the time and working collections for his father's business to see what he thought. Grandpa wrote back and said that times were tough and financially it wasn't working out well for him. He recommended Grandma take the job.

Grandma at her home in Rinard, Iowa. The steps led to the post office. Grandma invariably stood at the porch to wave us goodbye.

Grandma was required to take a governmental test in Fort Dodge with three other applicants. Dino Wagner's brother-in-law was one of them. He had been in the service which gave him bonus points on his exam. It was over 100 degrees in Fort Dodge with no air conditioning when she took the test. She never gave the kids any indication that she was concerned, though she must have been. Many in town didn't like the idea of someone from South Dakota coming in and taking a job from a local resident, especially when jobs were scarce. She did what she had to do. She got the job. It didn't pay much but it was consistent. Grandma, of course, stretched every dollar and raised her two children on what little she made. Mom and Uncle Harry never felt deprived or poor in any way.

Edythe Kunkle with a friend; Edythe is wearing a dress her brother, Ross Bachman, sent her.

With no Baptist churches in Nowlin, Grandma had joined the Methodist church and continued her Methodist affiliation in Rinard. On July 1, 1930, Grandma started her job as the postmistress of Rinard. The post office was initially next to Fisher's grocery store, and Grandma lived in a room behind the post office. Mom said it was a very meager living.

Grandma arrived in Rinard without any furniture. Her kitchen cupboard, sewing machine, washing machine, and trunk was sent from Lead after they arrived in Rinard. Aunt Mattie had a couch that opened into a single bed which she gave Grandma. She also gave her a kerosene stove with a portable oven that could be put on top of the burners. When coal was unloaded at the railroad, Harry collected strewn pieces free of charge for fuel. Corn was selling at 10 cents a bushel back then. Many farmers burned corn for heat!

Mattie and Fred Simpson

Rinard is situated a few miles from Lohrville where **EDYTHE LOUISE KUNKLE** would one-day work as an elementary teacher. She was also to meet a vital, young man who would one day become her husband, **CLEMENT FRANCIS CAVANAUGH**.

Until their washing machine arrived, Mom took the dirty clothes to Mattie's. Fred and Mattie had no children. Mattie's sister married an Ebers who had two children. Bill Ebers, Mattie's nephew, taught Mom how to play cribbage. Bill was a free spirit according to Mom and about 3-4 years older. He moved in with Mattie and Fred about the time Mom moved to Rinard. Mattie had a sister, Lucille, that was a nurse in Chicago. She had nice clothes and would send them to Mattie for Mom. Mattie also gave Grandma a round stove to heat the house. Years later, Mom gave me Mattie's 18-karat-gold ring for Julie's wedding band.

Grandma put $2.50 into a cup at the beginning of each week and discussed with Mom and Harry how it was to be spent. Harry often worked on a nearby farm, sometimes at Umbell's whose daughter, Dorothy, was a good friend of Mom's and would later retire and live in Greeley, Colorado. Dorothy's dad bought Uncle Harry a suit. Fobes was the superintendent in those days and gave Mom a job putting up signs advertising school events in exchange for a free ticket to the events.

When Ross and Glen's father died in 1939, Ross used his inheritance to buy Grandma the old Gaskill house in Rinard. Grandma moved the post office into her home next to the park. Her office was six feet in length and ten-feet-wide and served the town of 50 people. John Wetter was a local carpenter in town. They say John could look at what needed to be constructed and without measuring cut the boards to fit. He did the carpentry work turning Grandma's north porch into the town post office with a door that could be locked going into her living room.

Grandpa didn't own a car and wasn't able to keep in touch with the family very well after they

Edythe Kunkle at Wessington Springs her sophomore year of high school.

moved to Iowa. Mom recalled Grandpa taking her to a fair in Sioux City and riding the roller coaster together and how excited she was at the prospect of seeing him. On occasion, Mom also felt disappointed when his plans changed. We have a photograph of Grandpa, Grandma, Uncle Harry, and Mom in front of the Rinard post office. I believe it was the last photograph of the family taken together.

Shortly after that photograph was taken, Aunt Lizzie read in the Sioux City paper that Grandpa had robbed a bank. She broke the news to Grandma who, in turn, told Harry and Mom. Mom remembered going to church and singing "Faith of Our Fathers" and choking on those words. Grandma leaned upon her faith and friendship with Mattie and Andrew during those difficult times. I addressed that event in Part I.

During Mom's sophomore year of high school, she attended school at Wessington Springs, South Dakota, a Methodist school. Ross fronted the finances, and Mom paid him back. In retrospect, Mom thought it was extravagant, though at the time, she had some interest in going into nursing and thought that would help her career. In Glen's account, he wrote that Mom thought it would be easier to live out her Christian life if she attended Wessington Springs.

During Mom's first summer in Rinard, she babysat at Douty's farm three miles north of Rinard and a half mile west. Her pay was 50 cents a day. Mom spent summers and other times at Douty's much of her junior and senior year of high school.

Mom graduated from high school in 1934 and went to Morningside College in Sioux City for her two-year teaching certificate. Her first job was teaching at Lohrville. She moved there in 1936, the same year John Bachman died which was also the same year Grandma bought her home in Rinard. Until then, Grandma did not receive alimony or child support as her divorce with Bachman decreed. Ross wanted to protest the will for Grandma since she didn't get anything. Ross and Glen's father gave his estate to his sister Mary Rietz of Salem, South Dakota who had cared for him at the end of his life. The will stipulated that any protest would result in cutting off that heir's inheritance all together. For that reason, there was no protest and Ross and Glen each received an inheritance of $2,500 when their father died. Ross asked Glen if they could go together and use part of the money to help buy a home next to the Rinard Park for Grandma Kunkle. I understand that Genevieve, Uncle Glen's wife, vetoed that decision, perhaps necessarily so. Uncle Ross covered the cost of $1,200. Grandma paid Ross $5/month on a monthly income averaging about $30/month, her pay being based on the number of stamp cancellations, slim pickings for a town of 50. For Christmas, I would get a card with four quarters taped to it. She probably spent more money in December, but it was a better month for stamp sales.

Franklin Roosevelt signed the Social Security Act on August 14, 1935, and Social Security taxes were collected for the first time in January of 1937. Regular, ongoing payments began on January 1, 1940. Grandma's Social Security number was 482-60-2607. I don't believe Grandma received Social Security benefits but did receive some money from a post office pension initiated well into her career having appealed and being granted the ability to pay retroactively into her retirement fund.

Mom once shared with me that she was sleeping with Grandma one night and could hear her cry. Mom wished she had just given Grandma a big hug at that time. I believe Grandma's hugs were God-given as she trusted in Him for her needs, and her beloved Edythe was there as well.

Uncle Glen and Aunt Genevieve traveled to the New York World's Fair in 1939 with Grandma and Genevieve's parents. They journeyed through Ohio and visited many of Grandma's relatives that she kept in touch with. Grandma also visited her father's farm. She arrived at Ray and Minnie Shriver's home on July 9, 1939 in Caldwell, Ohio. They visited Mergeline Shriver Boyd at 622 No. 7ᵗʰ Street in Cambridge, Ohio. Mergeline Shriver's father, Dr. Frank Shriver, formally of Glenwood, Iowa was very low and died two days later.

Uncle Glen was an avid sports fan, and they attended the New York Yankees game where the great Lou Gerhig announced his retirement from baseball[36].

In visiting the world's fair Grandma wrote,

> We saw television. I wonder how soon that will become common? Tone light, neon lights, rapid spinning wheel, measure of weight of hand laid on piece of rail. Such fine and intricate instruments that would need study to understand. I wonder how they are thought up?

Grandma also became good friends with Grace Noel Crowell. I imagine she contacted her in appreciation for her many wonderful poems. Grace was born four years earlier than Grandma and died four years sooner. Uncle Ross financed a trip for Grandma to visit him in Hawai'i and routed her through Texas to visit Mrs. Crowell. She stayed a few days at her home. I unearthed a box of nearly 100 letters Grandma received from her. She was originally from Iowa, in fact, a few miles from Belle Plaine, but ultimately settled in Dallas, Texas where she remained until her death. She was selected as Texas's poet laureate. One famous poem of hers is,

To One in Sorrow

Let me come in where you are weeping, friend
And let me take your hand
I, who have known a sorrow such as yours,
Can understand

Let me come in - I would be very still
Beside you in your grief
I would not bid you cease your weeping, friend
Tears can bring relief

Let me come in - I would only breathe a prayer,
And hold your hand,
For I have known a sorrow such as yours,
And understand.

One day, I was looking up a hymn in a hymn book given to us from Julie's mom. To my surprise, one of the hymns was Grace Crowell's. I have a poem she wrote and autographed entitled, "Some One Had Prayed." Mom mentioned she memorized this poem of Mrs. Crowell's —

Some One Had Prayed

The day was long, the burden I had borne
Seemed heavier than I could longer bear,

*And then it lifted – but I did not know
Someone had knelt in prayer.*

*Had taken me to God that very hour,
And asked the easing of the load, and He,
In infinite compassion, had stooped down
And taken it from me.*

*We cannot tell how often as we pray
For some hurt one, bewildered and distressed,
The answer comes – but many times those hearts
Find sudden peace and rest.*

*Someone had prayed, and Faith, a reaching hand,
Took hold of God, and brought Him down that day!
So many, many hearts have need of prayer –
Oh, let us pray!*

After visiting Grace Noel Crowell, Grandma boarded a cruise ship for Hawai'i. It happened to be the same ship Uncle Paul Cavanaugh would take to New Guinea less than two years later, *The Lurline*.

After Mom and Dad's wedding on June 4, 1941, they honeymooned in the Badlands. On June 6, they received this letter from Grandma,

> My Dear Children,
>
> I am sorry I haven't written sooner but I found mail time on me before I realized it and then too late to write and reply. I left a write-up with Mrs. Easton (editor of the Lohrville paper). H. W. (Harry) and Arch were ready dressed for garden work when we left. Bernice Decker and Mrs. Earl Moore took me to Martens (Paul Marten in Mom's class). Miss Rasmussen played beautifully. They served 40 to a wonderful lunch. People said nice things about you and hoped for a happy life. Got Clem's card at noon. It is postmarked June 5, 5:30 and got here at noon today, the 6th. Please leave forwarding address at Lead and elsewhere. I sincerely hope you have a pleasant

safe trip. We wonder where you are "now" every little while.

God bless you both, Mother

Uncle Glen recalled that in 1945 Grandma became very sick with a gall bladder issue. Glen came and stayed at our home. One day, Grandma's condition was so bad Glen decided they better call Ross but when they called from our home phone, all the neighbors on our party line "rubbered in," as they called it, and they weren't able to get through to Uncle Ross. Today, it would be like all our neighbors taping into our Wi-Fi at the same time taking away our ability to get on the internet. Glen said Dad drove 100 mph to Lohrville where they placed the call directly from the telephone office. Ross did come as did "robust" Aunt Lizzie (as Glen described her) and Uncle Bert. Beloved Aunt Lizzie greeted Mom so loudly, the nurses cautioned her to be quieter because Grandma was so sick[37].

Grandpa hadn't seen or communicated with Grandma since being released from prison in 1939. He moved on with his life and later petitioned for a divorce which was secured in 1947. Grandpa and Grandma were married 33 years though together for 16 years. Mom remembers taking Grandma to the Rockwell City courthouse to file the paper work. Mr. Gray may have been the lawyer. Mom remembers going to the clerk's office with Grandma and asking the judge not to place the notice in the paper. They refused saying it must be public record. Grandma asked that Grandpa pay Ross back $12 for a bed, buffet, and dining room table she purchased from her nephew, Paul Jefferson, who needed money at the time. Grandpa did pay those expenses at interest, Mom recalls.

I remember Chris Siemann and I spending a few days at Grandma's. We went down to the railroad tracks and picked up railroad spikes and bought candy at Fisher's store. It was also fun hanging out at the park next door.

Grandma would sometimes visit us and stay in our downstairs guest room. I can still see her sitting at the vanity, the one Mom and Dad bought when they were first married and which sold at our

October 12, 2013 farm sale. Grandma combed out her long hair, braided it, and wrapped her braids into a bun. I recall sleeping with her one night and feeling needlessly uncomfortable when she pointed out the praying hands plaque on the wall and wondered if Grandpa had given that to us, she apparently knew. I said yes but didn't venture any further. There was a time when Grandma suffered a stroke and had slurred speech. I think Mom hoped I would sleep with Grandma during that time, but I didn't want to because I was afraid she might die in her sleep. I didn't want to tell Mom the reason for my reluctance, but Mom probed and I told her the next day why I didn't want to.

Grandma's 1941 journal sited she was with her family on New Year's Day. Those present wrote: "May this be the 'best' New Year, Love Edythe Louise"; "And many more of them, Love, Glen"; "May it be one that you will never forget. One whose joy is supreme, Clem"; "Full of health, wealth, and happiness, Genevieve." 1941 was a mixed bag. Grandma traveled to Hawai'i but also entered into her diary on Sunday, December 7, "Radio W.H.O. reported a Japanese attack on Pearl Harbor and Honolulu. Many killed and injured. Am concerned for Ross, Mildred, Ronald, and Russell and the many Hawaiian friends. All of this without warning." On December 8, Grandma entered, "Pres. Roosevelt asked the Houses to declare war against Japan (this after Japan declared war on us). Only Mrs. Rankin voted no. All others for war." Her entry on December 11, "Pres. Roosevelt asked Congress to declare war on Germany and Italy after many attacks on our ships. Mrs. Rankin did not vote, all others voted, yes."

Two men of note from Rinard who served in World War II were Dale Nuss and Robert Delanoit, both killed in action. Dale was inducted in August of 1942 and embarked on October, 1943. He served in England until June 6, 1944 when he participated in the D-Day invasion. He received the Presidential Unit Citation for making the landing on Normandy sometime in the first four hours of the assault and the Bronze Star with this citation,

> For meritorious service in direct support of combat operations from June 6, 1944 to April 11, 1945 in

France, Belgium and Germany. Sergeant Nuss performed his duties as Intelligence Sergeant in an exemplary manner. Through his initiative, sound judgment and devotion to duty, he contributed materially to the success of his unit in combat.

Harry Kunkle and Grandma in Rinard during his marine service in WWII

Nuss was killed in the Ruhrgebiet area of Germany on April 11, 1945 (Dusseldorf area) when his vehicle struck an enemy mine. The memorial stone in the Rinard park is dedicated to Nuss.

Also killed in action from Rinard was Robert (Bob) Delanoit. Delanoit was a senior in high school when his family moved from Rinard to Fort Dodge. His parents asked if he and his brother Paul could stay at Grandma Kunkle's for the last two months of their high school career. Uncle Harry was still living at home at the time. The Delanoit boys lived in the basement and cooked their own meals on an oven Grandma had in the basement. They slept on the couch. Robert's dad had been a pilot in WWI. His father was shell-shocked and often angry. Uncle Harry continued,

> I don't think he (Bob) ever dated. He played basketball and baseball. His dad had him working

most of the time. No social life. Good honest fellow. He apparently wanted to be a pilot like his dad had been. He was one of the few Catholics in town.

Bob was inducted on February 23, 1943 and embarked on August 19. He served in the China-Burma Theater as a pilot flying supplies with the 9th Combat Cargo over the Hump and Burma Road. Lieutenant Delanoit was killed in action while dropping supplies to the Marshall Task Force in Hpa-Lin Valley, approximately thirty-five miles north of Lashio, Burma. He is buried at Kalai Kunda, seventy miles from Calcutta, India.

Postmistress, Mary Kunkle, working at the post office located in her home

As with many small Iowa towns, those elements which helped the town grow eventually died off and the town's population with them. I think there were about 50 people in Rinard when I was a boy. In 1942, on the heels of a long depression and Rinard's decline, Mattie and Fred moved to Los Angeles where Fred secured a job after selling his hardware store in Rinard. Fred died in 1951 and Mattie returned to Rinard where she later married Ed Jones. In 1978, the Chicago Great Western made its last stop in Rinard.

Grandma began to prepare for her death. Grandma gave Mom an

envelope with various instructions in it for her funeral and final plans. There was a note to Mr. Bane,

> Dear Mrs. Bane,
>
> If the time comes for you to receive this. I want to ask a favor. Will you please select the appropriate hymns (your choice always has a message for the living) and sing them? Also, help the pianist to select hymn music for processional and recessional.
>
> Thanks, M. Kunkle.

Grandma requested the processional, *My Faith Looks Up to Thee* or any two hymns of Mrs. Bane's choosing. Reverend Bane was asked to do the obituary and sermon though Grandma outlived him. Reverend Everett Jarman of South Dakota (who helped Ross and Glen get into college) was asked to give a sermon as a backup to Bane. Grandma outlived him as well. Mrs. Nelle Johnson and Mrs., Florence Black were on the flower committee; Mr. H. C. Colie, Glen Smith, and Paul Stephenson were asked to usher; casket bearers included George Jones, Al Jones (Spud's dad and Ed's brother), Laurence Black, Eugene Parsons, Clell Early, Clarence Decker. The recessional song, "Nearer My God to Thee" with Alice Healy singing was chosen. Grandma also requested interment at the Oak Hill Cemetery in Belle Plaine and had her stone placed there. In Mom's envelop, Grandma included another note to "Susan," (her sister),

> Call Susan first and find out how to order preparation of cemetery lot. I have letters in safe from A. J., Elmer, Susan, and Lizzie turning their shares of the lot to me. I believe the cemetery is "Oak Hill." Please check and put it on the programs.

She later thought it would be easier for the family if she were interned at the Rinard cemetery. Mom shared how she took Grandma to Belle Plaine to retrieve her tombstone and put it in the trunk of the car. On the way through Perry, Iowa they stopped at Uncle Joe's. He had something for them and when he went to put it into the trunk of the car, he got a kick out of seeing Grandma's tombstone in the trunk.

Grandma included an obituary which she wrote:

> Mary Shriver Kunkle was born May 29, 1982 on a farm near Belle Plaine, Iowa. She was the 6th child of William and Martha Kirkpatrick Shriver. She was married June 4, 1902 to John H. Bachman. To this union were born Ross Bachman of Hawaii and Glen Bachman of Mitchell, South Dakota. Mr. Bachman is now deceased. She married Percy Kunkle December 29, 1913 and to this union were born Mrs. C. F. Cavanaugh (Edythe) of Lohrville, Iowa and Harry W. Kunkle of Des Moines. Besides are six grandchildren, a brother Elmer Shriver of Persia, Iowa sisters Mrs. Susan M. Beam, Luzerne, Iowa and Mrs. Lizzie Dillon of Ida Grove, Iowa. She united with the Baptist Church at Belle Plaine at the age of 12 years. After homesteading in South Dakota, she united with the Nowlin, South Dakota Methodist church as a charter member. Her membership was transferred to the Rinard Methodist church in 1930. Beginning 18th year as Rinard Postmaster. Brought first traveling library to Rinard in 1930. "Death is the star-lit pathway between the companionship of yesterday and the reunion of tomorrow."

Finally, Grandma included this note, "I owe Harry $150; Glen $25; Ross, hospital, nurses from August 30, 1947, $200. Pay both Bane and Jarman also Mrs. Bane $5; Dr. Isenberg for one lens and treating toe."

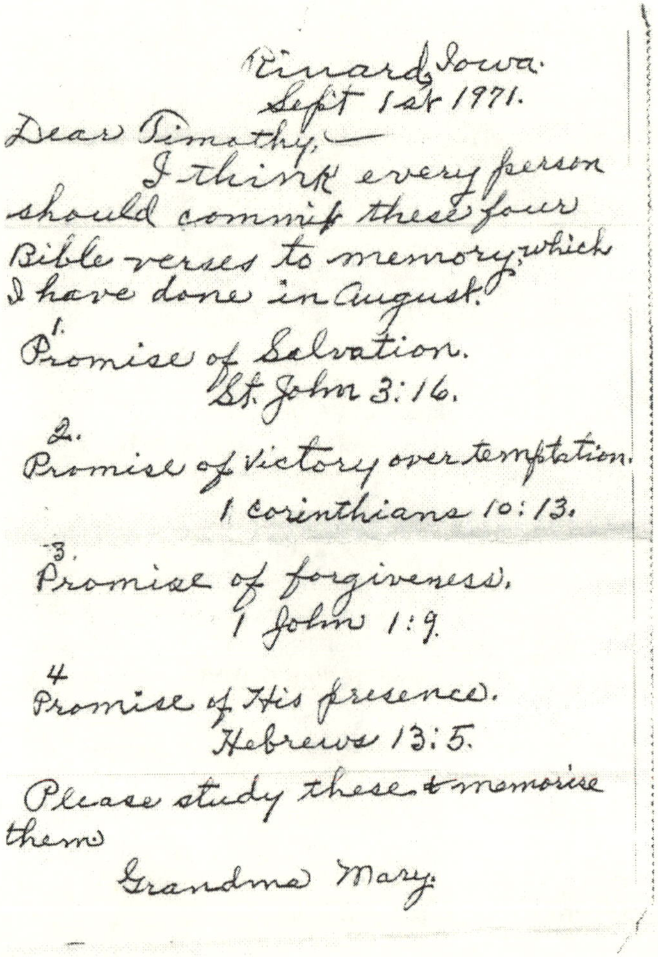

> Vinard, Iowa.
> Sept 1st 1971.
>
> Dear Timothy,—
>
> I think every person should commit these four Bible verses to memory, which I have done in August.
>
> 1. Promise of Salvation.
>   St. John 3:16.
> 2. Promise of Victory over temptation.
>   1 Corinthians 10:13.
> 3. Promise of forgiveness.
>   1 John 1:9.
> 4. Promise of His presence.
>   Hebrews 13:5.
>
> Please study these & memorize them
>
> Grandma Mary.

Grandma sent me the letter shown above weeks after I left for ISU. It means a lot to me now, but at the time I was embarrassed to get it.

In 1972, Grandma was operated on in Fort Dodge for cancer. I received a post card from Grandma dated September 27, 1972. She wrote,

Dear Grandson Tim,

Your note cheered me a lot. Not many college students could find time to write their Grandma Mary, thanks. I'm feeling better, but they are still taking tests. Food is ample and good. I'm sleeping well. Another x-ray tomorrow. I send my best regards to you, your parents, and all loved ones.

Grandma Mary

Grandma had a feeding tube placed through her nose into her stomach for a time. Mom remembers her pulling the tube out during the night and wondering if Grandma just wasn't cognizant of it. I've also wondered if, perhaps, Grandma knew exactly what she was doing and was just ready to depart and be with the Lord.

Grandma began to improve. Uncle Ross came from Hawai'i and Glen, Harry, and Mom were at Grandma's side for her final days in the hospital. The night before she was to be released, she had each of her children read selected passages from the Bible as she knit. She passed that night of a brain aneurism.

There was a tremendous blizzard the day of Grandma's funeral. Pat and Bonnie had stopped to pick me up at Alumni Hall but decided to turn around and return to Des Moines. One of the pall bearers couldn't make it so Uncle Cecil

Harry Kunkle, Mary Kunkle, Edythe Cavanaugh in Rinard, Iowa

filled in as an honorary pall bearer at Grandma's funeral.

Grandma lived in Rinard until her death in December of 1972. I visited her in the Lake City hospital when I was home from Iowa State at Thanksgiving time and recall kissing her on her forehead – which reminds me of her long, braided hair. I talked with Grandma briefly and that was the last time I saw her. Ross, Glen, Harry, and Mom were with her at the hospital the night before she passed. Grandma was 91-years-old, perhaps the last matriarch of the Shriver clan.

Within minutes of her death, a highway patrolman was speeding to Des Moines with Grandma's eyes in a cold sterile container. She donated them to the Lions Eye Bank, even though she had had cataracts in both eyes, they were still useful.

Uncle Ross followed her example and donated his body to the University of Hawai'i Medical School. After one year, he was cremated and his ashes strewn from an airplane over the Pacific Ocean. He died June 24, 1979 one month after I moved to Florida.

When Grandma died and the house sold, Ross wanted Mom to have the money from the sale of the house, but Mom sent it back to Ross. She thought it sold for about $2,500. Grandpa and Grandma Kunkle's estate, after expenses, were each, coincidentally, $600 at the time of their deaths.

I remember Grandma as a woman of faith, kind, sensible, hard-working, independent, content, frugal, community and progressive-minded, a lover of her children and grandchildren, well respected, beloved by many. She raised her four children primarily as a single mother and did a wonderful job. "Well done, Mary Shriver Bachman Kunkle!"

Left to Right: Glen Bachman, Mary Kunkle, Harry Kunkle, Edythe Kunkle, Ross Bachman

Appendix 1

Oaklands

After the death of his first wife, Harry Kunkle married Margaret (Maggie) Oakland, his first wife's in-home care giver. Margaret's father, **JOHANNES OAKLAND** (John Oakland) was born July 23, 1846 in Finaas Parsonage, Sondhordland, Norway. He was the son of **JOHANNES JOHNSON OKLAND** and **MARTHA NILSDAUGHTER OKLAND**.

John Oakland was baptized August 23, 1846 in the old Moster church which is one of Norway's oldest churches. With his mother passing when he was five-years-of-age, John's father did his best to raise his son according to Christian traditions. John was confirmed in 1861 at 15. On May 10, 1865, he and his sisters immigrated to the United States, sailing from Haugesund and landing at Quebec. John was 19. He and his sisters sailed the same vessel other Norwegian immigrants traveled on. Once the Norwegians immigrants, who became very close in their journey, arrived in the United States, they typically moved to one of three Norwegian settlements: Primrose, Wisconsin in Dane County; Leland, Illinois in La Salle County; and Benton County, Iowa. John made his way to Wisconsin and was employed for six months as a farm laborer near Madison and from there to Leland where he was

employed at farm work until the summer of 1866.

Jakob Mortvedt of Benton County, Iowa visited Norwegian friends in Wisconsin while John Oakland, then living in Illinois, was in Wisconsin visiting his sisters. Jakob encouraged John to return with him to Iowa. John decided to return with Jakob to Benton County, Iowa where he stayed several years. He was in Benton County when he became a citizen on April 25, 1868. It was there he married **MARTHE LARSDAUGHTGER PONSNESS** from Hjelmeland Parish, Norway, on February 29, 1869. The Lord blessed them with nine children. Two died in infancy and seven lived, including Mom's grandmother, Margaret, whose funeral I attended as an infant in Mom's arms.

One of John's sisters, Marina, was a very light-hearted woman but who married a very stern man that would punish her for her lighthearted ways, according to one account. She became guilt-ridden and experienced a nervous breakdown during her 40's. She was admitted into a mental institution in South Dakota. Even when the doctors felt she was well enough to leave, she chose to stay and worked there until her death.

In 1870, John and Marthe left Iowa to homestead in Clay County South Dakota where they lived for four years. Though raised a Christian, John was converted to Christ in 1872 while homesteading in South Dakota and from that time on, devoted his life to advance God's cause in the context of farming.

In 1874, he took up a preemption claim[38] in Turner County and lived there 35 years. He increased his holdings and became a farmer of nearly 500 acres of rich and productive land. From 1872 -1879 he suffered the loss of crops from grasshoppers and droughts. During one winter, he was without funds and as he expressed it, "I did not have enough money to buy a postage stamp." One year, he walked to Sioux City, Iowa, sixty miles to secure work and after an absence of three months from home, walked back the entire distance after having secured the needed money to provide for his family until spring. The only fuel he had for eight years was dry slough grass and hay, which was twisted into bundles and used for fuel. In 1881 there was no flour.

John Oakland, my great-great-grandfather, was known to bear these hardships with bravery and gradually worked his way to prosperity.

John Oakland became very involved in the South Dakota's Home Mission when it was founded in 1888. He became its administrator until his death. Immanuel Lutheran Church was built in 1898 with John Oakland one of its charter members and the superintendent of the Sunday school. He and John Johnson and Ole Ostrem went to Pierre and filed the declaration with the Secretary of State for organizing the church.

John Oakland retired to Centerville in 1905. Marthe enjoyed sitting in a rocker in front of the cook stove with the oven door open to keep warm. She didn't want people to know she smoked a clay pipe, so sewed a pocket inside her skirt to hide it. I've been told my great-grandma Leonard did the same thing. Maybe it was unique to that generation! The children laughed at their Norwegian Grandma when they found out the 90 pounds, five-feet tall grandmother was only human too[39].

Marthe died April 3, 1907 from pneumonia. Her obituary reads,

> The funeral services occurred Sunday, April seventh; from the house at one o'clock. L. A. Vadheim of Garretson opened the services with prayer and few sympathizing words in the Norwegian language. After the home service, they went to Immanuel Church five miles southwest of town, where a large assembly was already gathered. Her remains were taken to the Norwegian cemetery one mile and a half from the church until, 'The hour is coming, in which all that are in the graves shall hear His voice, and shall come forth: they that have done good unto the resurrection of life; and they that have done evil, unto the resurrection of damnation', John 5:23-29. John published a thank-you in the paper for the love and support shown his family, 'We wish to express our great appreciation and thanks for the evidences of deep sympathy and kind assistance in our great bereavement, the sickness and death of our beloved wife and mother'.

John submitted this article to the local newspaper after her funeral,

> The minister talked about Enoch who lived with God and whom God took unto himself, and about what St. Paul says, 'For me to live is Christ and to die is gain'. Her favorite hymn, 'A Holy Life, a Blessed Death, Each Other Lovingly Meet' was sung in the church. She was from Hjelmelands Parish in Norway and came to America with her parents in 1868. She was married to the undersigned in 1869 in Benton County, Iowa. Marthe came to an awakening and was converted over 35-years-ago (1872). She was under all trials been given grace to cling to Jesus' words and promises until she could finish her race. Dear friends, it hurts, when a faithful marriage partner is taken away from one in death after 40 years of sharing life's joys and sorrows together.

After his wife's death John traveled unceasingly for two years to further God's Word which was his greatest desire. On July 21, 1909, he married the widow of the deceased Pastor O. E. Torgerson. John and his wife moved into Irene in 1910, and on November 12, 1910, he suffered a stroke which paralyzed his right arm and leg. He learned to write with his left hand and continued to write profusely. One account reported,

> Mr. Oakland is a republican in his political belief, and he is identified with the Lutheran church in which he has served as a lay minister. Through the greater part of his residence he has been closely identified with church and Sunday school work and has been instrumental in organizing many church societies and Sunday schools in the state. He is a man of high ideals and noble purposes, has given a large portion of his time to the effort of inculcating a higher sense of duty and responsibility in both young and old.

On June 5, 1916, he suffered a relapse and lost the ability to speak but retained his senses to the last and died on Saturday morning, June 10, 1916. John Oakland was 69-years-old and 10 months when he passed[40]. He is buried in the Holland Cemetery located just west of Centerville, South Dakota. I took Mom there and met several Oakland relatives.

Ponsnesses

Front Row, Left to Right: John and Marthe (nee Ponsness) Oakland (my second-great grandparents); Lars and Serena Ponsness (my third-great grandparents); Martha Margarite and her husband, Andrew Braland, of Story City, Iowa; Back Row: Jens, Peter, Lars and wife. The Paola, Kansas relatives descend from Lars' son, Jonas.

Punt is the name for a grass with high tops and narrow, tight sitting leaves near the root. The last syllable of 'Ponsness' refers to the place where the farm was placed and means headland or point. 'Ponsness', then, literally means, "The farm which is placed on the headland where the punt is blooming."

LARS JONASSEN PONSNESS was born on July 28, 1818 in Fister overhus (outside of/farm), Norway. He and his wife are pictured above (my third-great grandparents). Lars was baptized August 16. His father was **JONAS BERGESEN OVERHAUS PONSNESS** (baptized July 9, 1775) and mother **MARTHA SJURSDATTER** of Riveland (baptized March 5, 1775; married in 1802). Martha Sjursdatter was probably the daughter of **SIVER** or **SJUR LARSEN** from the Riveland farm in Ardal (1738-1818) and his wife, **SIRI**

SEBJORNSDATTER (1751-1833).

The next generation back on Lars Ponsness' side was **LARS SIVERTSON VIGLESDAL** of Drittland who died in 1776 and who married **ANNA ADERSDAUGHTER**. Lars Siverton Viglesdal's father was **SJUR**, and his mother was **ASA**. Siri's parents were **SEBJORN SVEINSON EGLAND** who died in 1779, and who married the widow, **BERTE LARSDATTER (1711-1771)**.

Returning to Lars Jonassen Ponsness, pictured above, he married **MARGARET PEDERSDATTER SEGEDAL**. In the picture above, her name was stated as "Serena." She is probably the grandmother Grandpa Percy Kunkle referred to on page 88 and who lived in Rutland, Iowa (near Belle Plaine and in Benton County). She lived to be 105-years-of-age. Grandpa said he last saw her when he was 10 (1902), and she was 84 at that time, which would put her birth in 1818 - consistent with her actual birth year of 1819.

Lar's wife, Margaret Pedersdatter, was born July 26, 1819. Her mother's name was **MARGRETHE BERJESDAUGHTER SEGEDAL**, baptized April 28, 1782, and her father was **PEDER OLSEN SEGEDAL,** baptized February, 1781. Segadal was also written Segdal and Segredal and Zegredal. The name stems from "luxurious meadow."

Segadal lies remote from the highway and far from people. In the summer, it is possible to get to it either by land or sea. During the winter, when dangerous ice covers the fjord or snow covers the little path to Vadla, it is not so easy to be in touch with the world. The Segadal inlet is a good fishing place where they have had valuable brisling herring runs. They also mined feldspar and iron. Lead can be found in the mountain.

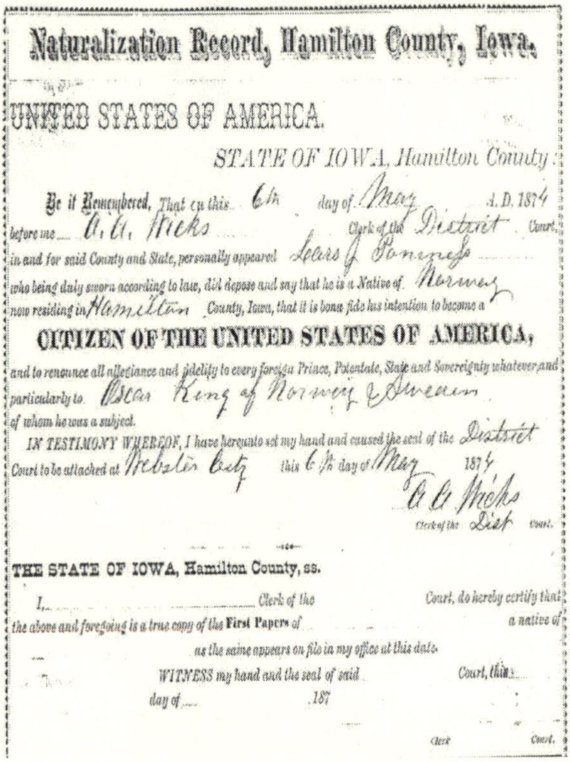
Naturalization Record, Hamilton County, Iowa.

UNITED STATES OF AMERICA.

STATE OF IOWA, Hamilton County :

Be it Remembered, That on this 6th day of May A.D. 1874 before me O. A. Wicks Clerk of the District Court, in and for said County and State, personally appeared Lars J. Ponsness who being duly sworn according to law, did depose and say that he is a Native of Norway now residing in Hamilton County, Iowa, that it is bona fide his intention to become a

CITIZEN OF THE UNITED STATES OF AMERICA,

and to renounce all allegiance and fidelity to every foreign Prince, Potentate, State and Sovereignty whatever, and particularly to Oscar King of Norway & Sweden of whom he was a subject.

IN TESTIMONY WHEREOF, I have hereunto set my hand and caused the seal of the District Court to be attached at Webster City this 6th day of May 1874

O. A. Wicks
Clerk of the Dist Court.

THE STATE OF IOWA, Hamilton County, ss.

I, ________ Clerk of the ________ Court, do hereby certify that the above and foregoing is a true copy of the First Papers of ________ a native of ________ as the same appears on file in my office at this date.

WITNESS my hand and the seal of said ________ Court, this ________ day of ________ 187

________ Clerk ________ Court.

Lars Ponsness' citizenship certificate

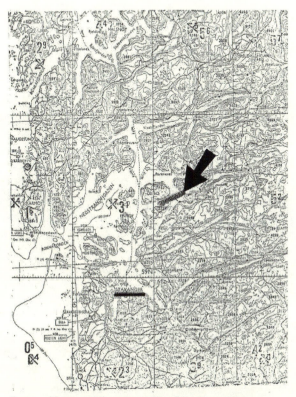

Ponsness' farm near the seaport City of Stavanger, Norway

John and Marthe Oakland's daughter, Margaret Oakland, Percy Kunkle's Norwegian mother. I attended my great-grandmother's funeral as an infant.

Percy and Mary Kunkle had four children: Ross Bachman, Glen Bachman (from Grandma's first marriage), Edythe Kunkle, and Harry Kunkle. Ross, Glen, and Edythe became educators; Harry, a veterinarian. Ross moved to Hawai'i nearly 30 years before statehood. He and Mildred had two sons, Ron and Russ. Glen remained in South Dakota his entire life. He and his wife, Genevieve, had three children: Jim, Barb, and Nancy. Edythe married Clem Cavanaugh, an Iowa farmer, and together they had four children: Mary, Pat, Sue, and Tim. Harry ultimately moved to Des Moines. He and his wife, Isabel, had four children: John, Marie, Bob, and Ted.

Mom was the 95-years-young, Matron of Honor at Lohrville Days in this photo. As I edit this account, she will be 102 on December 8, 2017, 278 years after Johannes Kunkle arrived in Philadelphia.

Appendix 2

Byerlys

JOHANN MICHAEL BYERLY was born in 1675 in Strassburg, Germany and arrived in America onboard the ship *Charming Nancy* on November 20, 1738. Johann's son, **ANDREW BYERLY**, my sixth-great grandfather, was born in Germany in 1715 and died in America in 1775 having arrived in Philadelphia aboard the *Charming Nancy* with his father. He would be the last of his Kunkle line to be born in Germany.

Andrew settled in Lancaster, Pennsylvania in 1745. His name appears as a purchaser of a lot on North Queen Street near Centre Square, October 25, 1745. It also appears in the Reformed Church records with his wife as sponsors for children baptized between February 3, 1745 and February 4, 1753 by pastors Schnorr, Vock, and Otterbein. Byerly appears at Fort Cumberland, Maryland, baking for the British army under the leadership of General Braddock in 1755. Here, with Major George Washington as a backer, he won a wager of 20 shillings in a foot race with a Catawba Indian warrior.

Andrew became baker for the British garrison at Fort Bedford, Pennsylvania, where his son Jacob was born in 1760. During 1759, Andrew was granted a tract of land on Bushy Run where he ultimately established a relay station between Fort Pitt and Fort Ligonier. Horses were changed every twenty miles at relay stations between the two forts. Andrew's family was living at Bushy Run when the Pontiac War of 1763-1764 suddenly broke out. Andrew became a key figure in the victory of the Battle of Bushy Run fought during the Pontiac War[41].

Andrew's first wife, Ann Catherine, died without issue. His second wife, **BEATRICE KUHL** immigrated to America with her father, **JOHN KUHL**. We don't know when Beatrice Kuhl was born, but we do know that she immigrated to Philadelphia on September 23, 1741. She and Andrew had five children: Frances, Catherine, Marie, Jacob, and our relative, Michael. After Beatrice died, Andrew remarried Phoebe Beatrice Gouldon of Rolle, Switzerland and had two more children.

Captain S. Ecuyer of Fort Pitt wrote a letter to Colonel Henry Bouquet on May 29, 1763 and warned of the great danger encompassing the Byerlys at Bushy Run. He warned that unless they left their house within four days, they would all be murdered. General Henry Boquet was good friends with Phoebe since they came from the same hometown in Switzerland.

While Andrew was away to help bury some massacred pioneer settlers, Phoebe received word of the impending attack in the middle of the night from a friendly Indian whom she had previously befriended[42].

Though Fort Pitt (Pittsburgh) would have been safer, the journey there was too difficult. Instead, Phoebe took her children and livestock through the woods in the dead of night to reach the closer, though less protected Fort Ligonier. With Indians in pursuit and on her heals, Phoebe safely brought her family to Fort Ligonier, a fort which played heavily into our family history.

In addition to the Byerlys, the Harmons also found refuge in the fort. **CHRISTIAN HARMON** (my 6-great grandfather; born 1728 and died 1785) and his wife, **CHRISTINA HARMON** (born 1728, died 1785) had three daughters: Magdaline, Maria, and Elizabeth. Christina helped Phoebe with the Fort's Sunday school classes. The Byerlys had three sons who met the three Harmon girls resulting in three marriages between the two families. Christina Harmon was a Dutch immigrant whose maiden name was Lenhart. We don't know who her parents were.

Christian Harmon was a private in the Lancaster County, Pennsylvania Militia according to the *1955 Year Book of the Pennsylvania Society, Sons of the American Revolution*, by Floyd G. Hoenstine qualifying us as Sons and Daughters of the American Revolution.

As Phoebe pursued safety, the men engaged in the Battle at Bushy Run. Colonel Bouquet would later relate that their thirst during the battle was more intolerable than enemy fire. The Indians had every advantage of being unencumbered and sheltered from the fire. The soldiers grew increasingly fatigued and distressed. The Indians anticipated a speedy triumph replete with scalps and goods as they derided the settlers in bad English. Kukyuskung, a Delaware chief who took part in murdering Colonel Clapham and his family, was the ringleader. His taunts were all the more provoking in that he often received many favors from Colonel Bouquet and the Royal Americans on his visits to Fort Pitt. The men in charge of the pack horses abandoned their watch and hid in the brush as packhorses bolted through the woods during the heat of battle. War whoops and confusion were everywhere. Chaos reigned.

It appeared that Bouquet's forces were near exhaustion when Captain Barret noticed a place where a large body of the boldest of the Indians might be taken on the flank and rear by a well-directed bayonet charge around the hill and up a ravine. Byerly was with Bouquet at the time and heard Barret's suggestion which the Colonel quickly put into action. Two companies were directed to bolt into the woods as one company was told to take their place in the front. Supposing the fleeing soldiers were retreating, the Indians all attacked the front only to be surprised by the flanking attack from the companies who "retreated" into the woods. Bouquet had them at last where he wanted them: in close quarters, with no dodging or popping from behind trees, and with his bayonets in place. The Indians fled past Captain Basset's second group who shot volleys at them. Many of their chiefs and soldiers were killed.

Cort, the author of *Colonel Henry Bouquet and His Campaigns of 1763 and 1764* recalled how his great-great grandfather, Jacob Byerly and his son, Joseph, shared a story with him on Christmas Day in 1855, just 2½ years before the old Revolutionary veteran passed away at the age of 99. Jacob related that his father, Andrew Byerly, shared how a Scotch Highlander dropped his musket as the battle turned in favor of the settlers and darted after one of the largest of the

Indians he could see. He soon captured him and returned him to the camp. He was met by an officer of Barret's detachment who asked, "What are you going to do with that Indian?" The Highlander replied, "I am taking him to Colonel Bouquet. If you want one, there are plenty of them running yonder in the woods and you may catch one for yourself." The officer drew his pistol and shot the prisoner through the head, which incensed the brave Highlander and called forth Bouquet's indignant rebuke when he was told of the incident.

Jacob Byerly was the last Revolutionary War veteran to die in Westmoreland County during his 99th year in 1858, just four years before Mom's uncle and Aunt Mattie's father, Andrew Shriver was born.

Jacob killed the notorious Indian chief, Kukyuskung, on an island in the Alleghany River in a campaign under Major Hardin in 1779. Kukyuskung tried to thwart peace efforts following the French and Indian War. He was one of the boldest and fiercest savages in assaulting the troops of Colonel Bouquet at the Battle of Bushy Run. He would stand behind a large tree and bellow out vulgar threats in broken English during the terrible night of August 5-6, 1763.

Bouquet won a decisive battle. Sixty dead Indians were found on the field, and many of the wounded had been conveyed away by their friends. Eight officers were killed or severely wounded and one hundred and fifteen men, or nearly one-quarter were missing as a result of the two-day conflict. The packhorse drivers emerged from the bushes and in company with some of the Rangers, proceeded to scalp the dead Indians. Bouquet reported that many of his men hated the Indians so much they would not even want to touch them to scalp them.

Many valuable goods were destroyed for lack of pack horses and not wanting them to fall into enemy hands. Litters were made, and the wounded were taken to Bushy Run where the army could rest and refresh themselves. Bouquet went on to Fort Pitt. From there he gave an ultimatum to the Indians that they must submit to his terms or be punished. He relieved Fort Pitt on August 20, 1763.

Rather than "burying the hatchet," which could be dug up again, the Indian leader, Red Hawk, said the hatchet would be thrown up to God that they might never see it again. Many white prisoners became so fond of Indian life that it was difficult to induce them to return to Christian homes. Mary Jemison, Rhoda Boyd, and Elizabeth Studibaker all returned to the Indians as wives and mothers. Bouquet required all captives returned and that the entire nation follow the chiefs' terms. Nettowhatways, the chief of the Turtle tribe refused to cooperate, and Bouquet deposed him and directed his tribe to elect another chief. One mother found a daughter who had been captured by the Indians nine years earlier. The child didn't recognize her mother. Boufort suggested she sing the German songs she used to sing to the child when she was a baby. Indeed, the daughter remembered her mother's songs.

The Battle of Bushy Run virtually established the supremacy of the Anglo-Saxon race in what would become America, not by British blood and valor alone but by the Swiss, Germans, and Scotch Highlanders.

Andrew died during a visit to Lancaster County, Pennsylvania just before the Revolutionary War.

Andrew's son, **MICHAEL BYERLY**, and Michael's wife, **MARIE HARMON**, were born in 1748 and 1762 respectively and died in 1827 and 1848 respectively. Michael's brothers, Frances and Jacob, both married two of Marie's sisters, Magdalena and Elizabeth (respectively).

Appendix 3

Lenharts and Harmons

Christian Lenhart Sr.'s log cabin built in 1782 on Farnsworth Road in Wilkins Township, Pennsylvania

CHRISTIAN PETER LENHART SR. immigrated to America and settled in Wilkins Township, Allegheny County, Pennsylvania in 1774, where he married **ELIZABETH HARMON**. Christian was born in 1748 and died in 1810. Christian was a scout for General Forbes during the French and Indian Wars and was an ensign in the 3rd Company, 8th Battalion, County Lancaster. He was granted 342 acres.

Christian's son, **ABRAHAM LENHART**, married Michael and Marie Byerly's daughter, **SARAH BYERLY**[43] in 1804. Other children of Michael and Marie were: Joseph, George, Elizabeth, Phoebe, Christina, Susan, Mary, and Ann. According to the *Cyclopedia of Westmoreland County, Pennsylvania*, by John M. Gresham and CO., page 397, "Abraham Lenhart was born in Allegheny County about the time of the Revolutionary War. He remained there following his occupation of farming until about 1820."

Lenharts, Harmons, and Byerlys were part of our early American family tree. We're related doubly to the Lenharts and Harmons, German and Dutch immigrants.

These families converged into one ancestor, Sarah P. Lenhart, the daughter of Abraham and Sarah (Byerly) Lenhart, the grandmother of Mom's grandfather, Harry Kunkle. Sarah Lenhart was born April 4, 1812 and died July 13, 1891.

Abraham and Sarah Lenhart's daughter, **SARAH LENHART**, married **JACOB PETER KUNKLE**. Abraham Lenhart's brother, UNKNOWN, also became one of my fourth-great grandparents whose daughter, **ESTHER LENHART**, married an Irish immigrant named **JOSEPH STEWART**. So, Esther and Sarah were first cousins. Esther's daughter, **HANNAH EMMA STEWART** married **JOSEPH KUNKLE**, the son of Jacob and Sarah Kunkle making them second cousins. It also made Abraham's father and mother, Christian and Elizabeth Lenhart, my double-fifth grandparents.

Harry Kunkle, Mom's grandfather, said that his parents, Joseph and Hannah, didn't realize until after their marriage that they were second cousins.

	Christian Lenhart/Elizabeth Harmon (Double-Fifth Grandparents)		
	Abraham Lenhart m. Sarah Byerly	Unknown Lenhart m. Unknown	
	Sarah Lenhart m. Jacob Peter Kunkle	Joseph Stewart m. Esther Lenhart	
	Joseph Kunkle (Son of Sarah/Jacob) m. Hannah Stewart (Daughter of Joseph and Esther)		

Appendix 4

Sons and Daughters of the American Revolution

The National Society of the Sons of the American Revolution (SAR) are based in Louisville, Kentucky and are centered around the purpose of,

> ... maintaining and extending the institutions of American freedom, an appreciation for true patriotism, a respect for our national symbols, the value of American citizenship and the unifying force of *e pluribus unum* that has created, from the people of many nations, one nation and one people.

The SAR comprises male descendants of ancestors who served in or contributed to the establishment of the United States of America. It was founded in April 30, 1889 by William Osborn McDowell. McDowell also contributed to the establishment of the Daughters of the American Revolution in 1890 (DAR).

We had several relatives on Mom's side that served in the Revolutionary War (Christian Harmon, Christian Lenhart Sr., and Michael Byerly). For the purposes of applying for the Sons and Daughters of the American Revolution, I used Michael Byerly, my fifth-great grandfather[44]. Michael's wife's father, Christian Harmon, also served in the Revolutionary War as a private in the Lancaster County militia. Paula Weber, a great-granddaughter of Joseph and Hannah (Stewart) Kunkle, sent me the documentation for the later generations of our lineage connecting us with Michael Byerly.

Paula writes,

> Michael Byerly signed the petition requesting Continental troops to be sent to Fort Walthour, Westmoreland County, Pennsylvania on 22 June, 1782. The petition was sent to General Irvine at Fort Pitt for military guard against Indian outrages. Michael Byerly is buried at Old Brush Creek Cemetery, Westmoreland County, Pennsylvania.

My genealogical link with two Revolutionary War veterans (Michael Byerly and Christian Harmon) qualifying our family as Sons and Daughters of the American Revolutionary War organizations are as follows:

Generation	Birth/Death/Marriage	City/State/County
(1) Michael Timothy Cavanaugh	b. February 15, 1953	Lake City, IA Calhoun County
	d.	
	m. November 28, 1981	Gainesville, FL Alachua County
Julie Ann Johnson	b. July 7, 1956	Emmetsburg, IA Palo Alto County
	d.	
Clement Francis Cavanaugh	b. January 25, 1916	Lohrville, IA Calhoun County
	d. October 18, 2001	Helena, MT Lewis & Clark County.
	m. June 4, 1941	Cedar, IA Greene County
(2) Edythe Louise Kunkle	b. December 8, 1915	Nowlin, SD Haakon County
	d.	
(3) John Percy Kunkle	b. October 2, 1881	Centerville, SD Turner County
	d. December 4, 1969	Chehalis, WA Lewis County
	m. December 29, 1914	Nowlin, SD Haakon County
		Belle Plaine, IA

Mary Shriver	b. May 29, 1882	Benton County
	d. December 10, 1972	Lake City, IA Calhoun County
(4) Harry Kunkle	b. October 16, 1865	Franklin, PA Vernango County
	d. March 15, 1945	Yankton, SD Yankton County
	m. 1889	Centerville, SD Turner County
Margaret Oakland	b. August 19, 1892	Clay County; SD
	d. November, 1953	Midland, SD Haakon County
(5) Joseph Jacob Kunkle	b. January 16, 1840	Irwin, PA Westmoreland County.
	d. January 20, 1908	Irwin, PA Westmoreland County.
	m. April, 1864	Clinton, PA Armstrong County
Hannah Emma Stewart	b. September 20, 1844	Clinton; Armstrong; PA
	d. October 9, 1921	Irwin, PA Westmoreland County.
Jacob Peter Kunkle	b. January 20, 1803	Westmoreland County, PA
	d. May 23, 1857	Harrison City, PA Westmoreland County.
	m. February 24, 1833	
(6) Sarah Lenhart	b. April 4, 1812	Westmoreland County, PA
	d. July 13, 1891	Westmoreland County, PA
Abraham Lenhart	b. March 11, 1782	Allegheny County; PA
	d. February 22, 1838	Westmoreland County, PA
	m. 1804	
(7) Sarah Byerly	b. January 17, 1783	Westmoreland County, PA
	d. December 9, 1848	Westmoreland County, PA
(8) Michael Byerly	b. December 7, 1748	Lancaster, PA Lancaster County

	d. July 22, 1829	Westmoreland County; PA
	m. 1779	Fort Walthour, PA Westmoreland County
(8b) Anna Maria Harmon	b. July 2, 1762	Lancaster, PA Lancaster County
	d. April 12, 1848	Westmoreland County, PA
(9b) Christian Harmon	b. 1728	Allegheny County, PA
	d. 1779	
	m. 1750	
(9b) Christina Lenhart	b. 1728	
	d. 1785	

The following documents were used to verify the accuracy of the genealogical information used to establish our Revolutionary, ancestral links:

Generation #5, Joseph Jacob Kunkle

Kunkle family Bible; 1880 Census Westmoreland County, PA, page 1034; Westmoreland County Book of Wills, #71; an Irwin Union Cemetery gravestone photo; and an obituary notice from Irwin newspaper.

Generation #6, Sarah Lenhart

Marriages and Deaths 1818-1865: Westmoreland County, PA, page 71; 1850 Census Westmoreland County, Vol. 3, page 30; Westmoreland County Books of Wills, Vol. 4, page 167; Adamsburg Cemetery gravestone photos; *Biography and Historical Cyclopedia of Westmoreland County*, page 397

Generation #7, Sarah Byerly

Biography and Historical Cyclopedia of

Westmoreland County, PA, page 397; Marriages and Deaths 1818-1865: Westmoreland County, PA, Vol. 1; page 106, 195; Old Brush Creek Cemetery gravestone photos; DAR #429921.

Generation #8, Michael Byerly
Trinity Lutheran Church Records, Vol. 1:1730-1767, page 65; Old Brush Creek Cemetery Gravestone photos; Westmoreland County Book of Wills, Vol. 2, page 209; Brush Creek Tales (Bomberger), page 46; DAR #759497.

The Daughters of the American Revolution require information on the children of the Revolutionary War ancestor chosen for the application. Michael and Anna Harmon's children were:

Sarah (our ancestor)	17 Jan 1782 d.	Abraham Lenhart
Christiana (Christina)	11 Mar 1792; d. 1877	Unmarried
Joseph	1783; d. 1865	Mary Smith
Mary	d. 1877	Joseph Kifer (Keiffer)
Susan (Susanna)	1798; d. 1882	Peter Iseman
George		Hannah Cort (Court)
Elizabeth		Fred Butler
Phebe (Pheby)		Fred Harmon
Ann M.	1823	Michael Baughman

Appendix 5

Wills

Jacob Kunkle

The last will and testament of Jacob P. Kunkle of the Township of North Huntingdon, in the County of Westmoreland. I Jacob P. Kunkle, considering the uncertainty of this mortal life, and being of sound mind and memory, do make and publish this my last will and testament, in the manner following:

First. I give and bequeath unto my beloved wife Sarah, the use of my farm, together with all the farming utensils, and household and kitchen furniture she needs for caring on the same, until my ... I also will and bequeath unto my wife for her use three head of horses, one brown mare, one gray mare, and also all the cows that are on the farm, also all the grain that is unsold in the barn, and in the ground, and all other personal property she needs for caring for the farm.

After my beloved wife Sarah has taken all the personal property she needs, then it is my will that my executors hereinafter appointed sell the balance at public sale, and

After paying all my just debts, funeral expenses, the balance of the money left to be put out and equally divided among my children hereafter named as they become of age: Maria, Joseph (our ancestor), Jacob R., John P., Sarah Ann, Rueben.

I will and bequeath to my second son, Jacob R. Kunkle when he arrives at 21-years-of-age, the farm I now reside on together with all the buildings and improvement thereon ... the home is to be for Sarah's residence for her natural life or if she remains my widow. After he has the farm two years, he is to pay the other siblings an amount of $5,000 in manner following: my daughter Maria, to be paid in three annual payments, one thousand dollars to my son Joseph to be paid in three annual payments, to my son John P. Kunkle, one thousand dollars in three payments, and to my daughter, Sarah Ann Kunkle, one thousand dollars in three annual payments. And to my son Rueben Kunkle, one thousand dollars in three annual payments.

I also will and bequeath unto my son Jacob R. Kunkle, when he becomes of age the threshing machine, two sets of horse ... plough and harrow and also the grey mares colt, and one farm wagon, Jacob is to furnish his mother (after he gets possession of the farm, with feed for one horse beast, also feed and pasture for one cow, and furnish her with as much meat as she needs for her use ... also as much flour as she may need for her use.

I further will and bequeath to my beloved wife, one hundred dollars out of the first money that comes into the hands of my executors.

Jacob Shriver

In the name of God, Amen. I Jacob Shriver of the township of Whitely Greene county and state of Pennsylvania being somewhat weak of body but of sound and perfect mind and memory praised be to God for the same do make and ordain this my last will and testament in manner and form as follows: First, my will is that my just debts and funeral charges be paid and discharged. I hereby ... appoint my well beloved wife, Jane Shriver and my brother John Shriver jointly to be my executors of this my last will and testament Second, my will is that my well beloved wife shall enjoy my homestead place with the moveable property until her youngest child comes of age and thirdly my will is that I give and ... to my son Elijah Shriver four hundred Dollars and also I give and devise to my son Adam Shriver four hundred dollars and also I give and ... to my son Jacob Shriver one quarter section of land. I have on the Muddy Fork of Wills Creek adjoining lands of John Johnson and Sorel Mare ... bridle and so much more as will make his portion amount to four hundred dollars and also I authorize my executor to sell my plantation on ... Creek ... for my two sons Michael Shriver and John Shriver one quarter section of land for each of them and also I devise so much more to 3each of theme as will make their portion amount to Four hundred dollars as piece and I also give and devise to my two sons William Shriver (our ancestor) and Isaac Shriver all the home place to be equally divided between them at the dea3th of my beloved wife Jane Shriver by their praying my daughter Eleanor Shriver an equal portion with the other kids and fourthly my will is that after my boys got their portions as above I give and bequeath to my daughter Christina Jacobson forty dollars and also I give and bequeath to my daughter Sarah Shriver forty dollars and also my will is that my daughter Christina Jackson Margaret Jackson, Elizabeth Shriver, Sarah Shriver and Mary Shriver shall have an equal portion of my personal property after my two daughters Christina Jackson and Sarah Shriver get their forty dollars ... fifthly, my will is that I give and devise to my son William Shriver twenty dollars or a colt worth twenty dollars when he arrives at sixteen years of age which will be thirteenth day of April one thousand eight hundred and twenty one to be purchased by my executors for him out of my personal property. I do hereby revoke and make null void all other wills heretofore made by me either by writing or by word of mouth. In witness and testimony, whereof I have hereunto set my hand and affixed my seal this 8th day of January one thousand eight hundred and fifteen.

Ulrich Keener

In the year 1784, the sixth day of April to the beginning of this writing, I Ulrich Keener, make my testament and will over my estate and goods, and my deceased son John Keener his oldest daughter Elizabeth Keener I will 15 pounds ... to Keener have I given a place for his portion and to Elisabeth keener peter millers wife I will her 15 pounds and barbary ... I will five pounds and a block spotted cow and a block spotted heifer and a deep dish and four pewter plates six pewter spoons and a little iron pot and a spinning wheel and the over plus of the pewter and a frying pan and a ... and a pair of shears after my decease and to Boston Keener have I bill of sale my place for his portion and a bald Eagle horse two pair of ... a drawing knife and a ... plow, plow irons, single trees and a cook chair after my decease and that I have Ulrich Keener, David Keener, Peter Keener I have given so much that may be satisfied to see if anything is over that I Ulrich Keener have may be satisfied to see if ... illegible.

Appendix 6

James Goodwill's Passenger List

The *James Goodwill's* passenger list shows David Crockatt as Master. They sailed from Rotterdam, Holland and then on to Falmouth, England. They landed in Philadelphia on September 27, 1727. There are three "Kiener" names listed and it shows nine in the "Kiener" family. I assume Uhlrich was one of the six family members not mentioned by name. The ship passenger's list is as follows:

Name	# in family
Michael Sigrist	6
Michael Tanner	2
Joseph Schurgh	3
Hans Haggy	4
Juurgen Miller	5
Hans Leaman	5
Hans Langneker	2
Hendrich Aberlee	5
Raynard Jung	3
Jacob Wygart	2
Wm. Wygart	/
Tewart Leatherman	6
Hans Michel Kunts	4
Jung Michael Kunts	/
Ulrich Stoupher	6

Ulrich Zug	4
Peter Zug	4
Barthol. Sigrist	4
Abraham Aberholt	4
Jacob Fritz	3
Adam Kiener	9
Wm. Kiener	/
Hans Kiener	/
Christian Webber	4
Margaret Heislern	4
Jurg Zengh	2
Jacob Gangwyer	1
Hans Michael Fiedler	3
Philip Schaberger	5
Hendrich Wolfe	2
Jurgh Steiniger	7
Joseph Clap	14
Johan Adam Philple	/
Jurg Clap	/
Ludowigh Clap	/
Christian Miller	/
Jurg Coch	/
Jacob Walter, Senr	6
Jacob Walter, Junr	/
Christopher Kirchofe	5
Jacob Siegel	6
Jacob Gass,Senr,sick	6
Fredrich Gass	/
John Miller	9
Joseph Miller	/
Hans Miller	/
Jacob Arnet	3
Paul Hein	6
Hans Hein	/

Bastian Merree	1
Michael Lybert	3
Hendrich Schultz	1
Hans Foster	1

About the Author

Tim Cavanaugh grew up on the family farm his grandfather purchased in 1917 and a few miles from the farming accident that claimed his great-grandfather's life. He developed a love for his family heritage from an early age and discovered his ancestral home in Ireland. He made many trips to Ireland over the years and became good friends with many in his ancestral home of Kilmacow.

He graduated from Lohrville Community High School and entered Iowa State University in the fall of 1971. Upon graduating with a double major in Industrial Administration and Psychology, Tim worked with a Christian ministry on the campus for three years.

In 1979, Tim moved to the University of Florida to help establish a campus ministry which his sister and brother-in-law, Matt and Jan Gordon, still lead. While in Florida, he married Julie Johnson of Havelock, Iowa in 1981 and was ordained a pastor by the Great Commission Association of Churches in 1983.

Tim and his family moved to Denver, Colorado in 1988 to help establish Northside Community Church and received his Masters of Divinity degree from Denver Theological Seminary and later his doctorate in Family Counseling from Masters International School of Divinity.

He and Julie are the proud parents of six children and six grandchildren: Erin and Paul Pavlik (Jonah, Jude, Idelette, Morrow); Caitlyn and Luke Bergman (Margaret and Ben), Ryan, Christopher, William, and Fiona Cavanaugh.

Endnotes

[1] In Catholic doctrine, an indulgence is a means by which a person can reduce time spent in purgatory. Indulgences can be acquired through prayer and good deeds, but Leo X also allowed them to be purchased.

[2] Charles V was the last Holy Roman emperor to be coronated by a pope.

[3] The Spessart is a low, circular mountain range in northwestern Bavaria and southern Hesse. The Main River borders the region on three sides. Geiersberg Peak, the highest point in the Spessart, towers over the Main River Valley at 1,923 feet. This region is sparsely populated with two nature parks, the Barvarian Spessart and the Hessian Spessart. Aschaffenburg and Wuerzburg are two prominent towns in the area. The brown Spessart Oak is reknown for its tight, straight grain and is used for fine furniture. Often described as a "fairyland" with its giant trees, historical towns, and awesome trails. The Spessart is a tourist destination today.

[4] J. Hans and Elisabeth Ickus' children: Jacob was born between 1650-1655. He married a Katharina Uhl on June 29, 1676 and died on February 2, 1692; Johann Michael was born in the 1660's and married on November 29, 1690; Johann Sebastian (our relative) was baptized on February 18, 1675 and died on October 14, 1737 in Floersbach. He married Anna Catharina Samer on January 29, 1700; Johann Nikolas was born 1677 and married January 30, 1703 and died August 17, 1751; Johann Martin was baptized on September 21, 1679 and died in Floersbach on August 17, 1751; Hans and Elisabeth's sixth child, Anna Margarethe, was born May 25, 1684.

[5] Johann Sebastian and Anna Samer's children: Melchior was baptized November 5, 1700; Johann George was baptized March 19, 1702; Eva Elisabeth was baptized September 29, 1703; Anna Elisabeth, August 29, 1705; our relative, Johannes (Hans), was born in 1709, married February 5, 1732, and died in 1764 in Northhampton County Pennsylvania. Johannes immigrated to America with his wife, Anna Magdalena Kaiser (born 1711); Johann and Anna's sixth child, Johann Peter, never married but was born in

1712 and died on August 5, 1726 at the age of 14. Johann and Anna's seventh son, Lorenz, was killed by Indians in Northampton County, Pennsylvania in January of 1756 having married Anna Catharina Kaiser shortly after arriving to the United States on November 12, 1748, born in 1715; the youngest child, Johann Michael, was born April 19, 1719 in Floersbach.

[6] In 2002, I received a phone call from James Kunkle of Denver, Colorado. Jim introduced himself to me as my fifth cousin. He had dedicated his life to tracking every Kunkle that immigrated from Floersbach, 64 in all. Each was assigned a "Book." Our relative, Johannes Kunkle, was Book Four, being the fourth of the Kunkles to leave Floersbach. It was Jim that shared with me great detail of our Kunkle heritage. He welcomed my input on our branch of the Kunkle tree which he had little knowledge of.

[7] First born and our ancestor, Johannes (age 15; born January 2, 1733, married in 1758 to Anna Margaret Schnerr and died December 22, 1813); Johann Peter (age 12; born July 23, 1735; married April 23, 1762 and died March 27, 1796); Johann Lorenz, "Lawrence" (age 9; born February 3, 1738, married Catherine in Pennsylvania and died October 15, 1800); Adam George (age 7; born February 18, 1741, married Esther in Pennsylvania and died in 1811); Johann Michael (age 5; Born June 18, 1743, married Schittler and died August of 1796); and Anna Katharina (age 2; born September 25, 1745, married Heinrich Bachman in 1763 and died before 1800). Three more children were born in the New World: Christina (born 1748, married Fred Warner in 1772, died on March 24, 1827); Johann Adam (born July 15, 1750, married Marge Giltner in 1772 and died November 24, 1827); Anna Kina (born June 6, 1753, married in Pennsylvania, died before 1800).

[9] The *Patience* was first mentioned arriving in New York from London in November, 1740 and departing three weeks later for Europe. In July of 1747, it was ferrying rice from South Carolina to London when it was attacked by Spanish pirates a few days out of Charleston. The crew of 14 were not injured but the captain, Robert Brown, was killed. His brother, John Brown, lost his left hand. The ship was later recovered and put back into service with the one-handed John Brown commanding the ship for its Palatine voyages.

The *Patience* made annual voyages from Rotterdam to Philadelphia in 1748,

1749, 1750, 1751, and 1753. the *Patience* was consistently called a "ship" in the customs records, a term that referred to a specific type of rig in the eighteenth century - originally a three-mast with a course, topsail and top gallant sail on the fore and mainmasts and a lateen sail and square topsail on the mizzenmast. the *Patience* was a relatively small ship of 200 tons (though described in one record as 300 tons) but with a capacity of 260 to 270 passengers with a crew of 15 or 16 in what must have been severely cramped quarters. One source says it also sported eight guns.

[10] There were no US Dollars in 1749, but one British pound in 1750 was roughly equivalent to 132 pounds today. 132 pounds today is roughly $175. So, ten pounds in 1749 may have equaled nearly $1,750 in today's dollars. The oldest four Kunkles cost about $7,000; the next three, about $2,500; and the youngest, Anna Katharina, was free being just 2-years-old. In some cases, these costs were covered by those who purchased the passengers as indentured servants.

[11] Kunkle's diary shows death was a big part of life in the colonial period.

[12] Johannes and Anna (Schneed) Kunkle's children: Johann Lorenz born 1759 and died after 1832; Maria Magdelina born July 1, 1762, married Adam Brandhofer in 1792 and died August 3, 1846; Michael (Conkle) born December 27, 1764, married Susanna Cort and died on April 9, 1813; Catherine born 1766 and married Peter Hill; John born August 19, 1769, married Anna Steinerin in 1790 and died January 2, 1850; Johanne George born 1771 and married Esther Heffle; our relative Johann Peter born 1773, married Elizabeth Ruch in 1795 and died February 9, 1829 and is buried in the Old Brush Cemetery; John Sebastian born January 2, 1775, married Anna Walthour before 1796 and died January 4, 1865; John Adam was born Februay 11, 1777; Barbara was born February 10, 1779, married Frederich Cort and died December 12, 1850.

[13] Johann Peter Kunkle and Elizabeth Ruch's children: John Henry born February 21, 1796; Anna Maria born December 31, 1797, married November 25, 1824 to Simon Andrew; Johann Peter Jr. born September 12, 1799, married Maria Baughman in 1823; John Lorenz born April 17, 1801, married October 25, 1825 to Sarah Ann Baughman, died June 15, 1874; Jacob Peter (our relative) was born January 20, 1803, married February 24,

1833 to Sarah Byerley Lenhart, and died on May 23, 1857; Johannes was born December 22, 1804 and died March 15, 1838; Anna Elisabeth was born November 6, 1806; Daniel was born September 1, 1808, married Esther Wegley on September 1828 and died September 3, 1892 (buried at Saint Jacob Cemetery, PA); Margaretha was born May 16, 1810, married Phillip Bush and died on December 24, 1886; Sebastian was born around 1815, married Sarah Eleanor Grove in 1836 and died after 1870.

[14] Jacob and Sarah Kunkle's children were: Lewis David born November 16, 1834 and died on January 7, 1836; Elisa Jane was born September 5, 1835 and died November 9, 1854; Maria Kunkle was born November 27, 1837 and married Abram Kunkle around 1857, she died in 1900; Joseph Jeremiah (our relative) was born on August 23, 1842 in Westmorland County, married Hannah Emma Stewart in April of 1864 in Armstrong County, died January 20, 1928 (Mom was 13 years old when he passed; he outlived all of his siblings); Jacob Rush was born August 23, 1842, married Annie Bickerstaff in 1878 and died on April 27, 1884; John Peter was born March 29, 1845 and married an Emma Leah, died in 1869; Sarah Ann was born on November 6, 1847, married John McCormick on October 3, 1870 and died on June 16, 1926; Reuben was born on December 10, 1851, was married February 28, 1880 to Elizabeth Jackson and died in 1911.

[15] Lida was Harry Kunkle's sister-in-law, the wife of his brother Taylor.

[16] Joseph Jeremiah and Hannah Emma Stewart's children were: Harry born October 16, 1865 in Franklin Township, Westmorland County; married Margaret J. Oakland in 1889 in Centerville, South Dakota; died March 15, 1946 in Yankton, South Dakota (our relatives); Edward born May 18, 1867 in Irwin, PA, married Annie Suffolk and died on December 9, 1944; Charles was born November 27, 1869, married Phoebe Landis and died August 30, 1941; Joseph George was born on March 24, 1871 and died November 15, 1941 in Saint Paul, Minnesota; Jacob Taylor was born September 1, 1873, married Lida Louisa Brown on October 11, 1911 and died August 15, 1964 (Sarah Forsmark was Taylor and Lida's daughter pictured with Joseph and Hannah in my photo of them. Sarah's daughter, Paula Weber, has completed the paper work to qualify our family as Sons and Daughters of the American Revolution); Jane L. was born February 22, 1875, married "Ede" before 1900, and died June 27, 1934; Emma K. was born June 10, 1877,

married James Whitney and died in North Dakota in 1972; Mary Mae was born October 3, 1880, never married and died on September 6, 1890; Pearl was born December 6, 1883, married Harry Stough and died on July 2, 1974.

[17] In the South Dakota Census of 1905 (Card #'s 862-868), Harry Kunkle of Centerville is listed as 40. Maggie was 32 and listed as a housekeeper. His occupation posted as a collector, and he was listed as having been in South Dakota for 17 years, which means he arrived in South Dakota in 1888 suggesting he did meet and marry his first wife in Ohio before coming to South Dakota and then marrying the second time, one year later.

[18] Harry and Margaret Oakland's children: John "Percy" born October 2, 1890 in Centerville (our relative), married December 29, 1914 in Rapid City South Dakota to Mary Shriver-Bachman, and died December 4, 1969 in Chehalis, Washington; Emma Mamie "Ruth" was born March 1892 in Centerville, married Ray Noble, and died in 1971; "Lillie" Louise was born October of 1894 in Centerville, never married, and died in 1989 in Sioux Falls, South Dakota (buried in Nowlin); William "Montrose" was born June 7, 1902 in Centerville, married Esther Lake in 1924, and died on January 7, 1988; Taylor was born in Centerville in 1905, never married, and died in 1931; "George" Washington was born February 22, 1908 in Nowlin, married Amelia Sorenson, and died in 1977; "Richard" Harold or "Birdie" was born in Nowlin in 1911, married Leona Burns on November 19, 1914, and died in 1974.

[19] Lake Louise in Alberta, Canada

[20] Bill Sands was in prison for 3 life sentences at 19-years-of-age. 30 years later, he was a successful businessman and acclaimed speaker as he shared his redemptive story of faith in Christ. I have Grandpa's autographed copy of Bill Sands' autobiography.

[21] Donald Cole was assigned as Grandpa's parole guarantor.

[22] In a ship fitter ad promotion, we read, "From a ship's smallest pieces to largest, a shipfitter cuts, grinds, fits, aligns, and tac welds large shield plates. You're building a ship. This job is only found in ship yards. It requires a lot

of physical strength ... hot in summer and cold in winter ... 'Steal Bangers' lift heavy objects in physically challenging areas: extreme heights, cramped quarters, on ladders. Welding is an important part of the job. There's a lot of climbing, some falling and crawling into compartments. Shipfitters sand and grind all day, tac weld and burn all day."

[23] *Scattergood Baines* is the "shrewd and jovial hardware merchant who finds himself drawn into just about everything that happens around him. Scattergood Baines is the best loved, most cussed at, and by all odds the fattest man in the modern, bustling town of Coldriver." *Scattergood Baines* offers down home wisdom to anyone that will offer him a plate of food as he is the fattest man in town. As the local hardware merchant, the town's locals come to Scattergood with their wild assortment of stories, problems, and backgrounds. The character Scattergood Baines was created by famous American author Clarence Budington Kelland.

[24] Kentucky became known as the "Promised Land" of vast animal herds; hidden treasures; lost silver mines; cheap, fertile, abundant land." Virginia passed primogeniture laws which required the oldest son to inherit their father's property. Younger sons were forced to seek their fortunes, most in Kentucky. Many Revolutionary War veterans received service bounty lands there. But the great migrations into Kentucky prior to 1825 reversed after that date, so much so, that Kentucky ultimately was a place people migrated through rather than stayed in.

[25] Allegheny Mountains are the west, central portion of the Appalachian Mountains.

[26] Ulrich's Will: Fayette County, PA, Will Book I, Pages 12 and 13

[27] Jacob was born in 1759 and married Elizabeth Shull December 2, 1783. John was born in 1763, married Alice Richards February 21, 1786, and died May 3, 1831. He is buried at the Shriver Cemetery, Whitely Township, Greene County Pennsylvania. His second wife was Sarah White. Abraham was born September 6, 1768, married Mary Keckley March 3, 1791. Died November 11, 1837. He is buried near Prentiss in Monongalia County, West Virginia. Catherine was born 1770 and married Peter Henkins March 3, 1789 and died August 24, 1842. Elizabeth was born in 1772 and married a Paterson on an undetermined date. She died in 1883. There may have been

a George and a Henry but we're not able to determine that for sure.

[28] Margaret Roxenia Jackson was born in Greene County, PA in 1806. She died March 25, 1868 and is buried at the Oak Hill Cemetery in Belle Plaine. She apparently had moved there to live with her daughter, Martha, and son-in-law, William Shriver, Grandma Kunkle's parents. Their children were: Jacob, Hannah Jane, Rachel, Martha, and Elizabeth.

[29] Hard Shell Baptist or Primitive Baptists trace their origins back to 1832 when, under the leadership of Gilbert Beebe, they severed their fellowship with "Mission Baptists." Priding themselves in following the New Testament exclusively. They rejected seminaries, mission societies, infant baptism, Sunday schools (preferring to place the spiritual education upon the shoulders of parents), temperance societies, tithing, and musical instruments. They originated in the mountainous regions of southeastern United States. Holding strongly to the 5-Point Calvinist position, they believed in predestination and, for that reason, rejected sharing the gospel thinking that would wrongly place the onus of salvation on the shoulders of man rather than on God. Well known Hard Shell Baptists included Abraham Lincoln's parents. After moving from Kentucky, the Lincolns settled on Little Pigeon Creek in what was then Warwick County, Indiana Territory and attended a church founded there on June 8, 1816 called the Pigeon Creek Church. When the meeting house was built, its site was selected about a mile west of Thomas Lincoln's home. Church records bound in deer skin reveal that on June 1, 1823, Thomas Lincoln and his wife Sally Bush Johnson joined the church. When Lincoln's mother died, she was buried between their home and the church, since the graveyard had not been established at that time. When Lincoln's sister, Sarah Grigsby died in 1828, she was buried in the church cemetery where her grave can still be seen today, marked with a rough stone. Some believe Lincoln's adult spiritual life was somewhat detached because of watching the fights and church splits among the Hard-Shell Baptists as a young man. It seemed to take the Civil War to draw him back to God. Understanding the Hard-Shell Baptist beliefs gives us insights into Henry Jackson Jr.'s life and explains why, in *Our Kith and Kin*, he is described as a strong singer and having family devotions.

[30] Jacob and Elizabeth's first son, Elijah, was born in 1784 and married Nancy – one of Henry and Hannah Jackson's kids; Christina born in 1786

also married a Jackson; Adam born in 1788 married a Gordon; Margaret born in 1789 married a Jackson; Jacob born in 1793 married a Patterson; Abraham born in 1791 never married; Elizabeth born in 1795 married a Patterson; our ancestor, Michael, born in 1797 married Susan Johnson in 1818; Sarah born in 1799 married a Jackson; Mary born in 1801 married a Jackson.

[31] John Glenn was born in Cambridge, Ohio on July 18, 1921. In 1939, he entered Muskingum College in New Concord and during his junior year left to be a US Marine Corps pilot in World War II. He flew 59 missions supporting ground troops. During the Korean War, he flew 90 combat missions and shot down three Migs (Communist planes). He earned five Distinguished Flying Crosses and 19 Air Medals. He also set a record, as a test pilot, flying from Los Angeles to New York City in 3 hours and 23 minutes breaking the previous record by over 20 minutes flying as fast as a bullet. In 1959, he went into the Mercury program, along with six other men. Their goal was to put an American into space, becoming the first astronauts of the United States space program. He was the third human being into outer space and the second (first American) to orbit the earth in Friendship 7. He helped lay the foundation for putting a man on the moon. In 1964 he resigned from the astronaut program to run for Senate but an inner ear injury required he pull out. He ran again in 1970 and was defeated but won the seat in the 1974 election. In 1984 he ran for the Democratic presidential nomination but discontinued his bid after early caucus losses. Lou Miller said she wrote to Mrs. Michael Cramer of 718 Audubon Drive, St. Louis, Mo. 63105. Mrs. Cramer's picture is in Kith and Kin as a girl scout. Her name was Lorena Deckman. She sent us the info we needed to link with Glenn via Lou. I wrote Glenn at The John Glenn Institute at the Ohio State University; 100 Bricker Hall; 190 North Ovall Mall; Columbus, OH 43210 and received a letter back from Senator Glenn verifying our relationship. We later met him at the Tattered Cover Bookstore in Denver, as pictured above.

[32] Grandma's sister, Aunt Lizzie (Amanda Elizabeth Shriver) was born in Persia 1876 and died 1948. She married John Dillon who was born 1870 and died in 1950. They are buried at Ida Grove, Iowa and had six children: Ed, Hazel, Zanther, Sybil, Merlin, and Mary. Hazel Marie married a Krick and would be the only one of the kids to stay in Ida Grove. Jennie or Eunice Shriver is buried in Belle Plaine as is Andrew Shriver's first wife, Ella, and his

second wife, Mrs. Anna Jane Spence, who lived with him in Rinard and passed of cancer.

[33] "The West Half of the Southwest Quarter of Section Twenty-Five in Township Seventy-Eight, North of Range ... of the Fifth Prime Meridian."

[34] Joe Leonard, 319-361-7357; joebphs65@gmail.

[35] The General Land Office (GLO) was created in 1812 and ultimately became the Bureau of Land Management on July 16, 1946. The GLO oversaw the surveying, platting, and sale of public lands in the Western United States and administered the Homestead Act and the Preemption Act which granted ownership to people already living on certain Federal properties.

[36] July 4, 1939 was declared "Lou Gerhig's Appreciation Day" in which Gerhig announced his retirement in a ceremony conducted between games of a double header with the Washington Senators. First basement, Gerhig, played 2,130 consecutive games holding that record 56 years until broken by Cal Ripken in 1996. Gerhig also held the most grand slams (23) of any player, a record that stood for 75 years until broken by Alex Rodriguez in 2013. Lou Gerhig was remembered that day for his famous, "I'm the Luckiest Man on the Face of the Earth" speech. He died two years later at the age of 38.

[37] Barbara Reardin gave me a copy of Uncle Glen's journal which I've extracted information most pertinent to our family history. He also wrote of Genevieve's nephew joining WWII and rising to the ranks of a Colonel. After the war, Genevieve's nephew gave George McGovern flight lessons. McGovern also attended Dakota Wesleyan and knew Glen well enough that after a faculty member left in 1952, McGovern called Glen and asked him to return to teaching at Dakota Wesleyan.

Glen's son, Jim, was on the election committee that succeeded in electing Tom Brokaw of Yankton as that year's Boys' State Governor. Brokaw appointed Jim as the Superintendent of Boys' State schools. In the military, Jim was responsible for maintenance of F-14s at Miramar Naval Air Base near San Diego. The 30-million-dollar plane had bugs in it requiring Jim and his crew to take it apart. He helped rewrite its manual. He was later sent to

Iran to help them learn how to fly the F-14s they bought from the United States.

Glen said one of his happiest memories was his visit to Iowa to our farm. Apparently, he was exhausted at work and came to recuperate at our place. Dad borrowed a pony, Spotty, from Winkelman's for the kids to ride while they were at our home.

When Genevieve was diagnosed with cancer, Glen recalled her saying, "I'm not better than anyone else." Glen choked to which Genevieve responded, "It's all right, Dad." In anguish Glen repeated, "I love you. I love you. I love you." Mom was notified by Glen as soon as Genevieve passed.

[38] The Federal Preemption Act was approved on September 4, 1841 during John Tyler's presidency. It allowed individuals to acquire federal land and claim it as their own. To preserve ownership, the claimant had to meet certain requirements to legitimize their claim. One requirement was to be actively residing on the land and another was to be consistently working to improve the land (for a minimum of five years). It was not necessary that the claimant be titled to the land; living there and working toward improving the stake was enough. If, however, the land remained idle for six months, the government could step in and take the property back.

[39] Marthe Ponsness' parents were **LARS JONASSEN PONSNESS** from the Fister farm Ovrehus and **MARGRETA PEDERSDAUGHTER SEGEDAL (SIRENE)** born in Hjelmeland parish on 7/27/1819. Lars was born 7/28/1818 in Fister. His parents were **JONAS BERGESEN** Ovre Fister (baptized 7/9/1775) and mother was **MARTHA SJURSDAUGHTER** Riveland, born 3/5/1775. Margrete Pedersdaughter Segedal's parents were **PEDER OLSEN SEGEDAL**, baptized July, 1781, and her mother was **MARGRETHE BERGESDAUGHTER SEGEDAL** born 4/28/1782. Their children were Jens, 4/5/1845; Marthe, 12/14/1847; Peder, 1/4/1851; Jonas, 3/16/1852; Martha Margrethe, 4/19/1854; and Lars, 5/30/1855. Marthe's brothers were Jens, Peter, Lars and her sister, Martha Margarite. Her sister married Andrew Braland of Story City, Iowa. The Paola, Kansas relatives descend from her brother Lars' son, Jonas.

[40] 4909 Sherwood Road; Madison, WI 53711, Gerhard Naeseth; Bjorn Moestue; H. J. Kogstads vei 2040 Klofta, Norway; Barb Hines, 921 Foster,

Sioux Falls, SD, 57103, 605-338-5229; Gladys Ponsness, Route 3, Box 274, Paola, KS, 66071; Stanley Knudson, 341 Dakota Street, Box 450, Centerville, SD, 57014.

[41] The Pontiac War began in 1763 out of dissatisfaction a collection of Native American Indian tribes had toward British policy following the British victory in the French and Indian War, a war to determine supremacy in the New World. The leader in the Pontiac War was Ottawa Chief, Pontiac.

[42] Several books give a greater detail of events that transpired including, *The Flight of the Byerley* and a book published in 1883 on Colonel Henry Bouquet and his campaigns of 1763 and 1764 in the Pontiac War.

[43] Sarah was born 1/17/1783, died 12/9/1843; Abraham was born 3/1/1782 and died 2/22/1858.

[44] I chose Michael because Paula F. Werber, my second cousin once removed, chose him and did much of the work required for the DAR and SAR applications. Paula's address is: 8000 Plum Creek Drive; Gaithersburg, MD; 20882.

ORDER COPIES OF

The Patience

online at

Amazon.com

Also available in ebook!

Made in the USA
Middletown, DE
12 June 2024

55633837R00139